REA's Books A

They have rescued lots of grades and more!

(a sample of the <u>hundreds of letters</u> REA receives each year)

"Your books are great! They are very helpful, and have upped my grade in every class. Thank you for such a great product."
Student, Seattle, WA

"Your book has really helped me sharpen my skills and improve my weak areas. Definitely will buy more."
Student, Buffalo, NY

"Compared to the other books that my fellow students had, your book was the most useful in helping me get a great score."
Student, North Hollywood, CA

"I really appreciate the help from your excellent book. Please keep up your great work."
Student, Albuquerque, NM

"Your book was such a better value and was so much more complete than anything your competition has produced (and I have them all)!"
Teacher, Virginia Beach, VA

(more on next page)

(continued from previous page)

" Your books have saved my GPA, and quite possibly my sanity.
My course grade is now an 'A', and I couldn't be happier."

Student, Winchester, IN

" These books are the best review books on the market.
They are fantastic!"

Student, New Orleans, LA

" Your book was responsible for my success on the exam. . . I
will look for REA the next time I need help."

Student, Chesterfield, MO

" I think it is the greatest study guide I have ever used!"

Student, Anchorage, AK

" I encourage others to buy REA because of their superiority.
Please continue to produce the best quality books on the market."

Student, San Jose, CA

" Just a short note to say thanks for the great support your book
gave me in helping me pass the test . . . I'm on my way to a
B.S. degree because of you !"

Student, Orlando, FL

Super Review®

All You Need to Know!

MICROECONOMICS

By the Staff of
Research & Education Association

Research & Education Association
Visit our website at
www.rea.com

Research & Education Association
61 Ethel Road West
Piscataway, New Jersey 08854
E-mail: info@rea.com

SUPER REVIEW®
OF MICROECONOMICS

Published 2009

Printed in the United States of America

Library of Congress Control Number 00-132719

ISBN 13: 978-0-87891-191-2
ISBN 10: 0-87891-191-X

What this Super Review® Will Do for You

REA's **Super Review** provides **all you need to know** to excel in class and succeed on midterms, finals, and even pop quizzes.

Think of this book as giving you access to your own private tutor. Here, right at your fingertips, is a brisk review to help you not only understand your textbook but also pick up where even some of the best lectures leave off.

Outstanding **Super Review** features include...

- Comprehensive yet concise coverage
- Targeted preparation for subject tests
- Easy-to-follow **Q** & **A** format that helps you master the subject matter
- End-of-chapter quizzes that provide pretest tune-up

We think you'll agree that, whether you're prepping for your next test or want to be a stronger contributor in class, **REA's Super Review** truly provides **all you need to know!**

Larry B. Kling
Super Review Program Director

CONTENTS

3   PRODUCTION—REVENUE AND COST

4   PERFECT COMPETITION

vii

5   THE MONOPOLY

6   MONOPOLISTIC COMPETITION AND OLIGOPOLIES

7 FACTOR PRICES

CHAPTER 1

Fundamentals of Supply and Demand

1.1 Economics and Scarcity

Economics is a social science that studies society's problem of choice among a limited amount of resources in its quest to attain the highest practical satisfaction of its unlimited wants. It is the allocation of scarce resources among competing ends.

Microeconomics focuses on problems specific to a household, firm, or industry, rather than those of a national or worldwide scale.

Scarcity is considered to be the basic problem of economics. Since all resources are limited in their availability, and society's desires for them are unlimited, there must exist some process of determining *what, how, how much*, and *for whom* to produce. Scarcity is the reason for the existence of price systems: as quantities of goods are limited, consumers must bid for desired goods.

Economic Goods are scarce and limited in their quantity; therefore, their prices are positive.

Free Goods are those goods that are not scarce. Their prices are zero because of their unlimited quantity. An example of a free good is air.

Problem Solving Examples:

 Define microeconomics.

 Microeconomics is the study of the behavior of individual components of the economy, such as firms, households or individuals, and the economic relationships among them. Microeconomics focuses upon individual, rather than aggregate, economic data. For example, a typical problem in microeconomics would be to determine the optimum price which a company should charge for a new product. In determining the solution to this problem, it would be necessary to consider such microeconomic data as the company's own production costs, the degree to which price changes affect the quantity demanded of the new product, and the prices which competing firms charge for similar products. Note that all of these data are specific to a particular firm or industry and to a particular product. In the example above, the conclusion which the company reaches regarding the optimum price for its product would not necessarily be the same for another company or another product. Nevertheless, the method of microeconomics can be consistently applied to a variety of problems in order to produce useful answers. For example, the same analysis of supply and demand relationships can be used to determine pricing policy in the automobile and garment industries, even though the specific supply and demand data for these industries may differ greatly.

 Define "scarcity" in economic terms. From what does economic scarcity result?

 Goods or resources are considered "scarce," in economic terms, if they are not available in sufficient quantity to satisfy all wants for them. Scarcity therefore results from a combination of two factors: quantities of goods are limited and desire for goods is unlimited. Since wants for virtually all goods are greater than the available supply, most resources are scarce. Only "free goods," such as air (in most situations), are not scarce.

1.2 Factors of Production

1.2.1 Definitions

Economic Resources and **factors of production** are the natural and unnatural inputs that are used in the production of goods and services. They fall into four general categories: land, labor, capital, and entrepreneurial talents.

1. **Land** is distinguishable as being fixed in its supply. It includes surface land, minerals, and other natural resources found in the air, soil, and sea.

2. **Labor** is composed of all human physical and mental abilities and qualities used in production of goods and services.

3. **Capital** includes produced goods, such as machines, buildings, and computers, etc., that are used as factor inputs for further production.

4. **Entrepreneurial Talent** involves human decision making, risk taking, invention, and ingenuity.

Problem Solving Example:

What is meant by "economic resources" or "factors of production"? Name three categories of resources.

Economic resources, also called factors of production, include all natural, artificial, and human resources which may be used in the production or provision of goods or services. For example, economic resources would include crude oil lying under the surface of the earth, the drilling and pumping equipment used to bring it to the surface, the pipeline which carries it to the dock, the ship (and its crew) which transports it to the refinery, the refinery and its workers and supervisors, the tank farm in which refined gasoline is stored, the truck (and its driver) which transports it to the service station, the service station at which it is sold to consumers (including the land on which it is situated, the building, and pumps), and the attendant who pumps it into customers' cars.

Three basic categories into which economic resources, or factors of production, may be classified are land, labor, and capital. Some economists (for example, McConnell) consider entrepreneurial ability, or "enterprise," to be a fourth category of economic resource.

1.2.2 Consumer Goods vs. Capital Goods

Consumer Goods directly satisfy the demands of the ultimate purchaser or consumer.

Capital Goods (real capital) indirectly satisfy consumer demands through their use in production of another good. Capital goods do not include money (financial capital). Money is not considered to be an economic resource.

Note: Some goods can be both consumer and capital goods.

Problem Solving Example:

Q Distinguish between consumer goods and capital goods. Is it possible for one good to be both a consumer and a capital good? Give an example.

A Consumer goods directly satisfy the wants or needs of consumers. Some examples of consumer goods are food, clothing and television sets. Capital goods satisfy consumer wants indirectly by their use in the production of consumer goods. Some examples of capital goods are tractors, textile looms, and machine tools.

It is possible for the same thing to be both a consumer and a capital good. For example, a farmer may own a pickup truck which he uses both to haul produce to market and for personal and family transportation. When the truck is used to haul produce it is a capital good, and when it is put to personal use it is a consumer good.

1.3 Opportunity Cost

The true cost of anything is the value of the next best thing which is given up because of that decision. **Opportunity Cost** stems from the foregone opportunities that are sacrificed in performing this certain action. For example, a tailor may be able to sew either a pair of pants or two shirts in an hour. If the tailor opts to make the pants, his opportunity cost will be the two shirts that could have been made in the same time.

Problem Solving Example:

 What is opportunity cost?

When resources are scarce, the decision to produce a particular good or service involves an opportunity cost, the sacrifice of a good or service that might have been produced instead. Opportunity cost describes the fact that when we employ resources in a particular way, we are not merely making a decision to produce these goods, but we are also deciding not to produce some other goods or services. That which we implicitly decide not to produce is the opportunity cost of what we do produce. Suppose a farmer has one acre of land, suitable for growing either corn or potatoes. If he plants corn, the opportunity cost of the corn is equal to one acre of potatoes. Because resources are limited, the production of any good necessarily involves an opportunity cost in terms of another.

1.4   Production Possibilities Frontier

The Production Possibilities Frontier Curve (PPF or PPC) or Transformation are names given to a way of illustrating the concepts of scarcity and opportunity cost. The curve defines the current limits on production capabilities in a given economic situation due to the physical restraints on resource supply and technology. It represents the maximum output combinations that are achievable under given market circumstances.

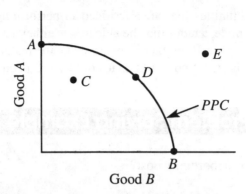

Figure 1.1 The Production Possibilities Curve

1. **On PPC**—the curve *ADB* represents the different production combinations of Good *A* and Good *B* that are possible in the economy under given market conditions if all the technology and other resources are being fully utilized. Furthermore, the economy displays full employment and maximum resource utilization along this curve.

    Point *A* represents the maximum of Good *A* that could be produced if all resources were directed for production of Good *A*. Point *B* represents the maximum of Good *B* that could be produced if all resources were directed for production of Good *B*.

2. **Inside PPC**—(i.e., point *C*) although it is technologically feasible to produce at point *C*, it involves underutilization of resources. More of Good *B* can be produced while still producing the same quantity of Good *A*.

3. **Outside PPC**—(i.e., point *E*) is an unattainable region of production given the current state of technology and resource supply.

$$\text{Slope of PPC} \ = \ \frac{MC_B}{MC_A} \ = \ \frac{P_B}{P_A}$$

where *MC* is marginal cost, and *P* is price.

1.4.1   PPC Properties

Shifts of PPC

Courses of Growth =   1. Improvement in technology
2. Increase in resource supply
3. Education

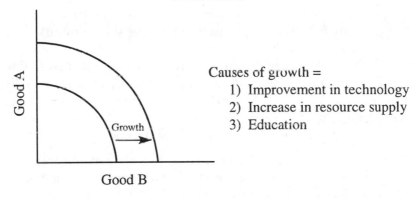

Causes of growth =
1) Improvement in technology
2) Increase in resource supply
3) Education

Figure 1.2

Let us assume that Good *A* is a **capital intensive** good (i.e., uses proportionately more capital than labor) and Good *B* is a **labor intensive** good (i.e., uses relatively more labor than capital). If the supply of capital increased and the supply of labor stayed the same, then the shift in the PPC curve will look like the shift in the graph depicted below.

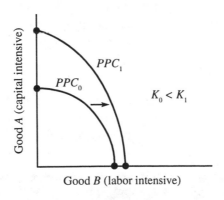

Figure 1.3 Shift in PPC Due to Increase in Capital

Note: Shifts **along** the PPC line **do not** represent a change in technology. Rather, they represent equally technologically efficient combinations of output from which to choose.

Problem Solving Example:

 Describe two ways in which an economy's production possibility frontier can be made to expand (or shift outward).

 An expansion, or shifting outward, of the production-possibility frontier indicates economic growth; that is, an increase in the economy's ability to produce goods and services. Two possible causes of economic growth are: (1) an increase in the available supply of factors of production or economic resources and (2) technological progress.

Expansion of economic resources can occur in a number of ways. For example, labor can be expanded both quantitatively, through population growth, and qualitatively, through education and training. Capital can be expanded through investment, which allows increased production of capital goods.

Technological progress also causes an expansion of the production-possibility frontier, because improved technology allows more efficient production using existing economic resources. For example, a breakthrough in solar energy technology would result in increased production of usable energy without requiring the increased depletion of existing raw materials, such as coal or oil, which could in turn be used to produce such goods as plastics or synthetic fibers.

1.4.2 Concavity of PPC

The PPC is usually drawn concave to the origin because inputs are, in general, not equally adaptable to alternative uses. The concavity of the PPC illustrates the Laws of Increasing Relative Costs and Diminishing Returns.

Problem Solving Example:

 Illustrate, using production possibilities curves:

a) the law of diminishing returns

b) a situation in which there are constant returns

c) a situation in which there are increasing returns.

A Diminishing returns describes a situation in which additional units of an input result in decreasing additional output. It is important to keep in mind that this situation exists when at least one other input is held constant. On a production possibility curve, the law of diminishing returns looks like this:

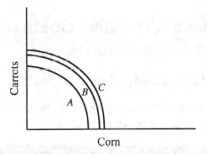

where curve *A*, *B*, and *C* each represent an equal increase in one input, say land. Notice the decreasing distance between the curves indicating a decline in additional output.

Constant returns describes a situation where an increase in all inputs brings about a proportionate increase in output. In such a situation, a doubling of inputs would result in a doubling of output, as in the figure on the left below:

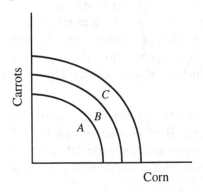

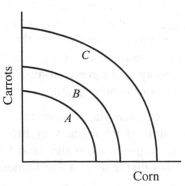

where curves *A*, *B*, and *C* represent equal increases in all inputs. Notice the equal distances between the curves, indicating a constant increase in output.

Increasing returns describes a situation in which an increase in all inputs brings about a proportionately greater increase in output, for example, a doubling of inputs causes output to triple. This situation is illustrated in the figure on the right, where *A*, *B*, and *C* represent equal increases in inputs.

Notice the increasing distance between the curves, indicating a growing rate in increase of output.

1.5 Increasing Relative Costs and Diminishing Returns

1.5.1 Law of Increasing Relative Costs

In order to get equal **extra** amounts of one good, you must give up an ever increasing amount of another good.

Problem Solving Example:

Q What is the law of increasing relative costs, and how does it relate to the law of diminishing returns? Illustrate the effect of the law of increasing relative costs on the shape of the production-possibility curve.

A The law of increasing relative costs applies when the factors of production required to produce one good are required in different proportions than for the production of another good. In such a case, in order to cause equal increases in production of one good, the economy will have to forego production of increasingly large increments of the other good.

For example, assume that automobile production requires large amounts of labor but very little land. Beef production, on the other hand, requires extensive land but comparatively little labor. Assume further that there is a fixed amount of land available which is suitable for grazing cattle. Finally, assume that, at the outset, the economy's entire labor force of 100,000 is engaged in automobile production, and that 12,000 automobiles per year are being produced.

Now assume that 10,000 workers are withdrawn from the automobile industry and employed in beef production; and, as a result, 2,000 additional head of cattle are produced at the expense of a decline in automobile production of 1,000 cars per year.

Suppose 10,000 additional workers are transferred to beef production. Because this additional labor input is being added to a fixed amount of land, the law of diminishing returns tells us that the additional labor input will result in a smaller increase in beef production (say 1,750 head) than resulted from the earlier increase in labor input of 10,000 workers. Moreover, the law of diminishing returns tells us, conversely, that the withdrawal of the second group of 10,000 laborers from the production of cars, causes a reduction in car production greater than that caused by the withdrawal of the first group of 10,000 laborers, say 1,250 cars. Thus, the transfer of the first 10,000 laborers from car production to cattle production resulted in an increase of 2,000 head of

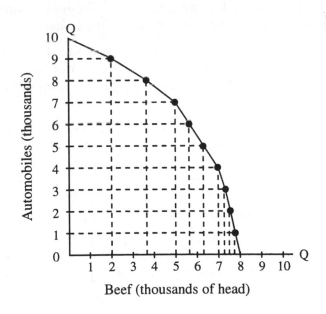

Beef (thousands of head)

cattle and a decrease of 1,000 cars, which means that the cost of each additional head of cattle, in terms of cars foregone, was 1,000 cars ÷ 2,000 head of cattle = 0.5 car per head of cattle. The cost of the second transfer of 10,000 laborers from car to cattle production was 1,250 cars and the gain 1,750 head of cattle, so that the cost, in terms of cars foregone, at the higher level of cattle production, is 1,250 cars ÷ 1,750 head of cattle ≅ 0.72 cars per head of cattle.

Each additional transfer of a group of 10,000 laborers from automobile to beef production will result in even greater decreases in automobile production, and successively smaller increases in beef production because of diminishing returns.

The law of increasing relative costs may, therefore, be said to be an outgrowth of the law of diminishing returns. It is important to remember that the law of increasing relative costs only applies where the goods in question require factors of production in different proportions or amounts. If, in the hypothetical example above, automobile and beef production required equal proportions of land and labor, each transfer of labor from automobile to beef production could have been accompanied by a proportionate transfer of land. Diminishing returns would not have set in and relative costs may not be increasing.

Where the law of increasing relative costs applies, the shape of the production-possibility curve will be convex, that is, bowed out away from the origin. The figure, which is based on the hypothetical example above, illustrates this.

The successively smaller increases in beef production resulting from equal decreases (note horizontal dashed lines) in automobile production can be seen in the decreasing distances (moving from left to right) between the vertical dashed lines.

1.5.2 Law of Diminishing Returns

If the input of some resource is increased while others are held constant, total output will increase, but at a decreasing rate. Eventually, the more you increase inputs beyond a certain point, output will actually decrease.

The Law of Diminishing Returns and the Law of Increasing Relative Costs are closely related.

Diminishing Returns + Scarcity $\Rightarrow$ Increasing Relative Cost

Note: The PPC is a straight line if and only if the relative cost is constant.

Problem Solving Example:

What is the law of diminishing returns? Give an example of its operation.

The law of diminishing returns states that, after a point, equal increases in the input of a factor of production, the input of other factors of production remaining fixed, will result in successively less additional output.

For example, a factory may have ten machines, each of which is operated by one worker. Hiring a second worker for each machine will allow the factory to add a second eight-hour shift and double production. A third worker per machine would similarly allow it to triple production by adding a third eight-hour shift. But any additional workers would only serve to relieve other workers during coffee and meal breaks, etc. This would result in a relatively small increase in output. Thus, diminishing returns would set in with the hiring of the thirty-first worker.

1.6   Changes of Scale—Returns and Economies

1.6.1   Shifts in the Scale of Production

Shifts in the Scale of Production occur when all inputs are being changed at the same time, and in the same proportion.

1.6.2   Returns to Scale

Diminishing Returns to Scale (DRS) occur when an increase in inputs leads to a less than proportionate increase in outputs. For example, if all inputs are doubled, the total output is **less** than doubled.

Constant Returns to Scale (CRS) occur when an increase in input leads to a proportionate increase in outputs. For example, if all inputs are doubled, the total output is doubled.

Increasing Returns to Scale (IRS) occur when an increase in inputs lead to a more than proportionate increase in outputs. For example, if all inputs are doubled, the total output is more than doubled.

1.6.3   Economies of Scale

Economies of Scale arise when the increase in output is more than proportionate to the increase in inputs. This can be a direct result of increasing returns to scale or occur due to the declining factor prices.

Diseconomies of Scale arise when the opposite scenario than the one above occurs.

Problem Solving Example:

What are "economies of scale," and how do they relate to the law of diminishing returns?

Economies of scale are increases in the engineering efficiency of production which result from increasing the scale of production, that is, increasing the quantity of all required inputs of production (capital, labor, land, etc.) in the same proportion. Doubling the amounts of all inputs may result in more than doubling output because of economies of scale. This results from a number of factors, including, for example, the ability to implement specialization and division of labor, and the possibility of using more technically efficient large-scale energy sources.

The principle of economies of scale does not contradict the Law of Diminishing Returns, because economies of scale result from increasing the inputs of all factors of production in the same proportion.

Diminishing returns result when one or more of the factors of production are held constant while others are increased, with the result that the factor proportions become different from what they were.

1.7 Markets—Supply and Demand

A **Market** is the interaction between potential buyers and sellers of goods and services, where money is usually used as the medium of exchange.

1.7.1 Demand

Demand for a good is the quantity of a good that consumers are willing and able to purchase at a certain price. The **Demand Curve** is the combination of quantity and price at all prices.

Problem Solving Example:

Define the term "demand" in economics. Give an example to illustrate demand.

Demand is defined as a schedule which shows the various amounts of a product which consumers are willing and able to purchase at each specific price in a set of possible prices during some specified period of time. Note the phrase, 'willing and able", because willingness alone is not effective in the market. One may be willing to buy a Mercedes-Benz, but if this willingness is not backed by the ability to buy, that is, by the necessary dollars, it will not be effective and, therefore will not be reflected in the market.

This table represents hypothetical data for an individual buyer's demand for corn.

Price per bushel	Quantity demanded per week
$5	10
4	20
3	35
2	55
1	80

The demand schedule in and of itself does not indicate which of the five possible prices will actually exist in the corn market. This depends on both demand and supply. Demand is simply a tabular statement of a buyer's plans, or intentions, with respect to the purchase of a product.

It is important to note that to be meaningful, the quantities demanded at each price must relate to some specific time period—a day, a week, a month, and so forth. The phrase "a consumer will buy 10 bushels of corn at $5 per bushel" is vague and meaningless. The phrase "a consumer will buy 10 bushels of corn per week at $5 per bushel," however, is clear and very meaningful.

1.7.2 Supply

Supply of a good is the quantity of that good that producers offer at a certain price. The collection of all such points for every price is called the **Supply Curve.**

> **Note:** 1. The quantity demanded and supplied of any good usually depends on the price of that good, but it also depends on a number of other determinants, which will be discussed shortly (see Section 1.7.4).
>
> 2. Desire is not the same thing as demand. In order to have a demand for a good, you must be **able** to purchase it, not just desire to purchase it.

1.7.3 Demand Curve

A demand curve depicts how the quantity demanded of a good changes as the price of that good changes, holding everything else constant.

Normally, as the price of a good increases, the quantity demanded of that good falls; this is known as a **normal good.** This can be shown as **movements along** the demand curve. This is known as the **Law of Demand.**

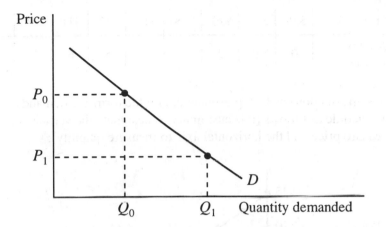

Figure 1.4 The Demand Curve

Problem Solving Example:

 What is meant by "demand" and what is a "demand curve"?

"Demand" refers to the relationship between quantity of a good that an individual or group desires and is able to buy at a particular time, and the price per unit of the good, factors other than price being equal. The desire to buy is not by itself sufficient to constitute demand: it must be accompanied by sufficient purchasing power.

The demand relationship can be viewed in either of two ways. It can be viewed as specifying the maximum quantity of a good that an individual or group desires and is able to purchase at a given price. Or, alternatively, it can be viewed as specifying the maximum price per unit that an individual or group of individuals is willing and able to pay for a given quantity of a good.

A "demand curve" is a graphic representation of this relationship between the quantity of a good demanded and the price of the good (other factors remaining constant). For example, let the following schedule represent Smith's demand for shirts on October 1st:

Price	$25	$22	$20	$18	$15	$12	$11	$9	$6
Quantity demanded	0	1	2	3	4	5	6	7	8

This information can be represented in graphic form as a demand curve or schedule as follows (it is customary to designate the vertical axis to measure price and the horizontal axis to measure quantity):

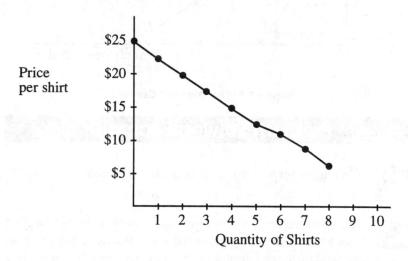

Here we have Smith's demand curve for shirt X on October 1st.

1.7.4 Shifts in the Demand Curve and Determinants of Demand

A change in any determinant of demand for a good, other than the price, will produce a shift in the demand curve. A shift to the right represents an increase in the demand for that good at each given price. This can be seen as the shift from D_0 to D_1 in Figure 1.5(a). A shift to the left represents a decrease in the demand for that good at each given price. This is seen as a shift from D_0 to D_2 in Figure 1.5(b).

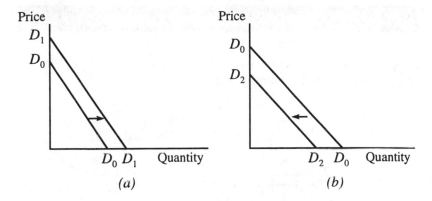

Figure 1.5 Shifts in the Demand Curve

There are a number of factors that can produce a shift in the demand curve:

1. **Consumer Income**—at any given price of a good, as Y (income) increases, the quantity demanded of a good **normally** increases.

2. **Population**—at any given price of a good, as population grows, quantity demanded of a good normally increases.

3. **Consumer Preferences**—at any given price of a good, if consumer tastes shift in favor of that particular good, there will be an increase in the demand for that good.

4. **Price and Availability of Related Goods**—a decrease in the price of **complementary goods** (such as tennis rackets and tennis balls) shifts the demand of our original good to the right. The opposite happens when the price of the complement increases. Decrease in the price of the goods which are **supplements** (as margarine is for butter) shifts the demand curve to the left. The opposite happens when the price of the supplements increases.

Problem Solving Example:

Q What is the difference between an increase in demand and an increase in the quantity demanded?

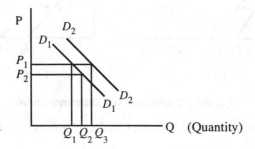

A An increase in quantity demanded is caused by a reduction in price. It involves movement along the demand curve. In the figure, using D_1D_1 as the demand curve, as price decreases from P_1 to P_2, quantity demanded increases from Q_1 to Q_2. The demand curve itself is unchanged, but a change in price has caused a change in the quantity demanded.

An increase in demand involves an actual shift of the entire demand curve to the right. At each price, a greater quantity is demanded than was previously demanded. It can be seen in the figure that along D_1D_1, at P_1, the quantity demanded is Q_1. But if demand increases to D_2D_2, at P_1, the quantity demanded increases to Q_3.

1.7.5 Supply Curve

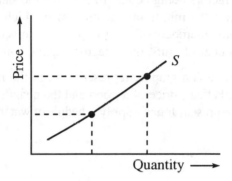

Figure 1.6 The Supply Curve

A **Supply Curve** depicts how the quantity supplied of some good changes during a specific period of time, as the price of that good changes, *ceteris paribus*.

Law of Supply—Normally, as the price of a good rises, the quantity supplied rises. This can be shown by the movement along the supply curve.

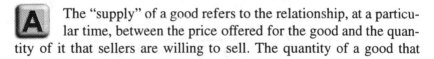

Problem Solving Example:

What is meant by the term "supply," and what is a "supply curve"?

The "supply" of a good refers to the relationship, at a particular time, between the price offered for the good and the quantity of it that sellers are willing to sell. The quantity of a good that an individual or group is willing to sell depends on the per-unit price of the good, other factors being equal. To describe the same relationship in a different way, the minimum per unit price which will induce an individual or some members of the group to sell units of the good depends on the number of units, other factors, again, being equal.

A supply curve is a graphic representation of the relationship between the (hypothetical) price of a good and the quantity supplied. Let the table below represent Jones' supply schedule of watermelons on July 4th:

Price	$1	$2	$3	$3.50	$4	$4.50	$5	$5.50	$6	$7	$8
Quantity	0	0	1	2	3	4	5	6	7	8	9

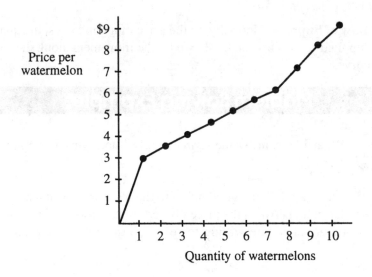

The information in the table can be presented in graphic form as Jones' supply curve, as shown in the figure above.

Problem Solving Example:

 State the law of supply.

The law of supply states that there is a direct relationship bettween price and quantity supplied. As price rises, the corresponding quantity supplied rises, and as price falls, the quantity supplied also falls. In other words, it simply states that producers are willing to produce and offer for sale more of their product at a high price than they are at a low price.

1.7.6 Shifts in the Supply Curve and Determinants of Supply

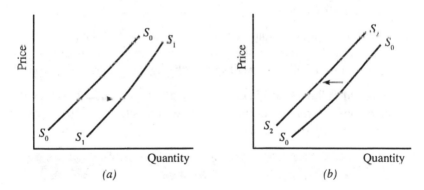

(a)   (b)

Figure 1.7 Shifts in the Supply Curve

A change in any determinant of supply for a good, other than the price of that good, will produce a shift of the supply curve. A shift to the right represents an increase in the supply for that good at each given price. This can be seen in Figure 1.7(a) as a shift from S_0 to S_1. A shift to the left represents a decrease in the supply for that good at each given price. This can be seen as a shift from S_0 to S_2 in the Figure 1.7(b).

There are a number of factors that can produce a shift in the supply curve, as opposed to movements along the supply curve which are caused by changes in the price of the good in question:

1. **Size of the Industry**—At any given price of a good, an increase in the size of the industry producing that good will shift the supply curve to the right, thus, increasing its supply.

2. **Technological Progress**—At any given price of a good, any technological progress in the production of that good will increase the supply for the good.

3. **Prices of Inputs**—At any given price of a good, if the prices of inputs, which are used in the production of this good, decrease, the supply curve of this good will shift to the right (an increase in supply).

4. **Price of Related Outputs**—At any given price of a good, as the prices of the related outputs increase, the supply of the good in question will also increase.

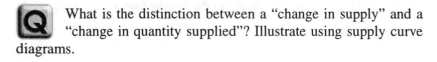

Problem Solving Example:

Q What is the distinction between a "change in supply" and a "change in quantity supplied"? Illustrate using supply curve diagrams.

A A supply curve represents the relationship between the quantity of a good that potential sellers will supply and the per unit price offered for the good, other factors remaining the same. A "change in supply" refers to a change in the relationship between the quantity of a good that suppliers are willing to sell and the per unit price of the

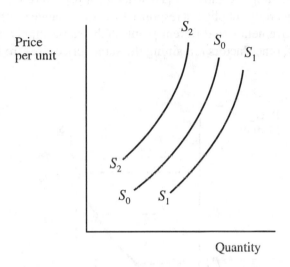

good due to a change in one of the factors which affect this relationship. That is, a change in supply means that at any given price sellers are willing to sell more or less than they were previously. A "change in supply" is represented graphically, therefore, by a change in the position of the supply curve, as illustrated in the figure.

If S_0S_0 represents the initial state of supply, an increase in supply is indicated by a rightward and downward shift in the supply curve, e.g., to S_1S_1. At any given price, a larger quantity will be supplied than initially at S_0S_0. Similarly, a leftward and upward shift in the supply curve e.g., to S_2S_2, indicates a decrease in supply, for, at any given price, a smaller quantity will be supplied than initially at S_0S_0.

If, on the other hand, the quantity of the good that will be supplied at each possible price remains unchanged, but price changes, the response to the price change is a "change in the quantity supplied." The set of different quantities that will be supplied at different prices, other factors remaining the same, is just what a supply curve represents. A change in quantity supplied in response to a price change is represented, then, by movement to a different point on the same supply curve. For example, if, other factors remaining the same, price rises from P_0 to P_1

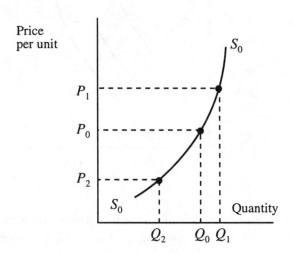

in the figure above, suppliers will supply a larger quantity, Q_1, as compared to Q_0 at P_0. Similarly, if the price falls from P_0 to P_2, suppliers will supply a smaller quantity, Q_2 as compared to Q_0 at P_0.

1.8 Equilibrium of Supply and Demand

1.8.1 Changes in Supply and Demand

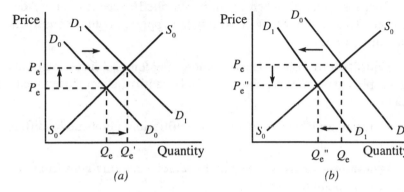

(a)   *(b)*

A– As $D\uparrow$ (increases) and S is fixed, Eq (equilibrium) P (price) $\uparrow$ and Eq Q (quantity) $\uparrow$.

B– As $D\downarrow$ and S is fixed, Eq $P\downarrow$ and Eq $Q\downarrow$.

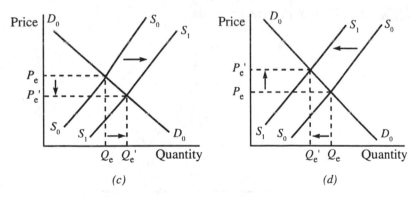

(c)   *(d)*

C– As $S\uparrow$ and D is fixed, Eq $P\downarrow$ and Eq $Q\uparrow$.

D– As $S\downarrow$ and D is fixed, Eq $P\uparrow$ and Eq $Q\downarrow$.

Figure 1.8 Shifts in Demand and Supply

Shortage—Occurs when quantity demanded exceeds quantity supplied. That is, consumers demand more than producers are willing to supply.

Surplus—Occurs when quantity supplied exceeds quantity demanded. That is, producers are willing to supply more than consumers are willing to buy.

Equilibrium Point—Occurs where the demand curve intersects the supply curve. At this point, price and quantity have no incentive to change.

Comparative Statics—Compare equilibrium points under different market circumstances.

Dynamics—Consider the path by which economy goes from one equilibrium point to another.

Problem Solving Example:

 Show graphically the effect of an increase in demand on equilibrium price and output.

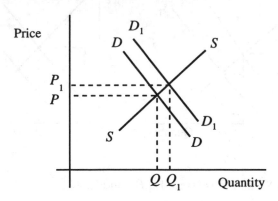

Consult the figure. As demand increases from DD to D_1D_1, quantity demanded increases from Q to Q_1, and price increases from P to P_1. Correspondingly, a decrease in demand will cause equilibrium price and output to decrease.

1.8.2 Marshallian and Walrasian Stable Equilibrium

Market price and quantity are determined by the intersection of the demand curve and supply curve in a free market economy. For example, the equilibrium price on the graph is P_e and the equilibrium quantity is Q_e. In our simple supply and demand diagram, any movement away from equilibrium will bring about correcting market forces which will cause a movement back to equilibrium. This is called a **stable equilibrium.** For example, if prices rise to P_2, as in the graph, the quantity supplied will be greater than the quantity demanded. Thus, we will have a surplus supply on the market. Suppliers will want to lower their price to get rid of this surplus and prices will fall back to P_e. If for some reason prices fell to P_1, demand would exceed supply and a supply shortage would occur. Consumers would bid prices back up to P_e. In the example, we moved price away from equilibrium and noted the correcting forces to get price back to equilibrium price. This stable equilibrium is called a **Walrasian equilibrium:** that is, price is the adjusting mechanism to get back to equilibrium.

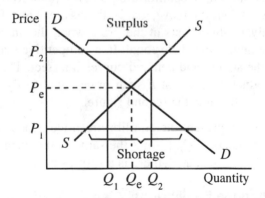

Figure 1.9 Supply–Demand Diagram

However, instead of looking at the price, suppose quantity were to move to Q_2. At Q_2, the supply price would be greater than the demand price; therefore, less trade would take place and the quantity will fall back to Q_e. The opposite scenario will happen if the quantity happens to be at Q_1. When we move quantity away from equilibrium quantity and note its return, we are observing **Marshallian equilibrium:** that is, we look at quantity as the adjusting mechanism to get back to equilibrium.

Problem Solving Example:

Q Given the supply and demand schedules for product A as shown, suppose that the price is currently P. Assuming that there are no price floors or ceilings, to what equilibrium price will this market tend?

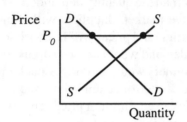 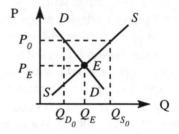

A By definition, an equilibrium point is a point from which there is no tendency to move, that is, things are at rest. In supply and demand analysis, this occurs at the price when the amount supplied and the amount demanded are equal. In a competitive market, this occurs where the supply and demand curves intersect. The equilibrium point for product A occurs at E with price equal to P_E and quantity equal to Q_E, as shown in the second figure.

P_0 does not represent the equilibrium price, since, at that price, the quantity demanded, Q_{D_0}, is not the same as the quantity supplied. $Q_{S_0} \times Q_{S_0} > Q_{D_0}$, so that, at P_0 there is a surplus of A.

1.8.3   Unstable Equilibrium

Suppose we have a backward bending supply curve as depicted in Figure 1.10. Although this type of curve is not common in the

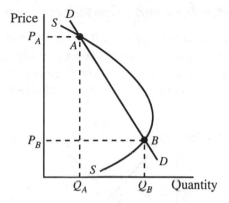

Figure 1.10 Unstable Equilibrium

economy, it can and does happen. Point *B* is our usually stable equilibrium where the supply curve intersects the demand curve. At a price slightly higher than P_B, we have a supply surplus and producers will lower their price back to P_B to clear the market. The reverse scenario can occur if prices were slightly below P_B.

However, point *A*, while an equilibrium point, is not stable. If for some reason prices were to change, market forces will not bring us back to the equilibrium point. For example, if price were to rise above P_A, demand would be greater than supply. So we would have a supply shortage. Due to this supply shortage, consumers will bid up prices to get the limited supply, causing prices to rise more. This trend will continue and we would not get back to equilibrium.

In the above discussion, we looked at price as the adjusting mechanism (Walrasian), but we could have just as easily looked at quantity as the adjustment mechanism (Marshallian). Walrasian equilibrium and Marshallian equilibrium are just flip sides of the same coin.

1.8.4   Price Ceilings and Price Floors

When market forces are permitted to interact freely, quantity demanded will equal quantity supplied (point E in Figure 1.11). A **price ceiling** occurs when prices are set **below** the equilibrium price by the government or some other non-market force. This price ceiling induces shortages, $Q_D - Q_S$.

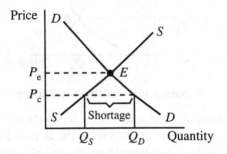

Figure 1.11 Price Ceiling

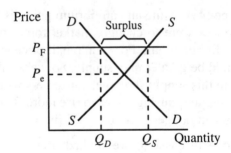

Figure 1.12 Price Floor

The support price for a good, a **price floor**, occurs when the government or some other non-market force pushes the price for that good higher than its equilibrium price. A price floor induces a supply surplus, $Q_S - Q_D$. This is depicted in Figure 1.12.

Problem Solving Example:

Q The government has set a price ceiling on cigarettes so that there is a shortage, as illustrated in the figure below. The tobacco industry complains to the government that the ceiling price is far below the equilibrium price. In response to their claims, the government, which does not have access to the figure, sends an economics student into the marketplace to investigate the situation. After a week of study, he concludes that since the quantity sold by the stores equals the quantity bought by consumers, the market is in equilibrium, and there is no need to reconsider the ceiling price. What is the fallacy in his argument?

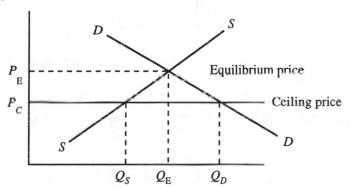

A The student is correct in saying that quantity sold = quantity bought. But this equality is true in any situation, no matter what the price. What the student fails to realize is that equilibrium occurs at that price at which the amount consumers are willing to buy is just matched by the amount producers are willing to sell. If the student had taken the correct approach to studying the market, he would have discovered the amount consumers are willing to buy at the ceiling price, Q_D, is considerably higher than the amount producers are willing to sell Q_S. The difference, $Q_D - Q_S$, represents the amount of the shortage. Although consumers demand the amount Q_D at price P_C, they can find only amount Q_S for sale at that price. So Q_S is the amount actually bought and sold, and the demand for the additional quantity $Q_D - Q_S$ goes unsatisfied. Thus the equality of the quantity bought and the quantity sold, which always exists, at any price, does not imply equality of the quantity demanded and the quantity supplied, which occurs only at the equilibrium price, P_E.

1.9 Elasticities

1.9.1 Coefficient of Price Elasticity for Supply and Demand

The coefficient of price elasticity for demand is:

$$\eta = \frac{\Delta Q / Q}{\Delta P / P} = \frac{\Delta Q}{\Delta P} \cdot \frac{P}{Q}$$

η measures the relative responsiveness of quantity demanded to a change in price.

The coefficient of price elasticity for supply is:

$$\varepsilon = \frac{\Delta Q / Q}{\Delta P / P} = \frac{\Delta Q}{\Delta P} \cdot \frac{P}{Q}$$

ε measures the relative responsiveness of quantity supplied to a change in price.

Note: Slope $\neq$ elasticity

$$\text{Slope} = \frac{\Delta P}{\Delta Q} \neq \frac{\Delta Q}{\Delta P} \cdot \frac{P}{Q} = \text{elasticity}$$

Problem Solving Example:

 What is the elasticity of demand?

The elasticity of demand is a measure of the extent to which quantity of a good demanded, Q, responds to changes in the price, P, of the good. Specifically,

$$\text{Elasticity, } E, = -\frac{\text{Percentage change in quantity demanded}}{\text{Percentage change in price}}$$

$$= \frac{1}{\eta}\frac{\Delta Q/Q}{\Delta P/P} = \frac{1}{\eta}\frac{\Delta Q}{\Delta P}\cdot\frac{P}{Q} \text{ ,}$$

where ΔP represents the change in the price of the good, and ΔQ represents the resulting change in the quantity of the good demanded.

1.9.2 Point vs. Arc Elasticity

Point Elasticity (ideal, preferred in principle) measures minute changes, so that asymmetries between %Δ in different directions is insignificant.

Arc Elasticity (used in practice) measures larger changes, and makes allowance by taking %Δ in relative to average between two points in consideration.

Midpoint Formula:

$$\eta = \frac{\Delta Q/\left[\frac{1}{2}(Q_1+Q_2)\right]}{\Delta P/\left[\frac{1}{2}(P_1+P_2)\right]} = \frac{\Delta Q/(Q_1+Q_2)}{\Delta P/(P_1+P_2)}$$

Problem Solving Example:

 What is the difference between arc elasticity and point elasticity? Use an example.

 To make easier the explanation of elasticities let us make use of the following demand function: $Q = 7 - P$. The following points are contained in that function

P	Q
4	3
3	4
2	5

Suppose we were asked to find the elasticity of the demand function on the interval $P = 2$ to $P = 4$. This elasticity between two points $(2,5)$ and $(4,3)$, is called arc elasticity. Let us use the midpoint formula for price elasticity of demand, as follows:

$$e = \frac{-\dfrac{Q_1 - Q_2}{Q_1 + Q_2}}{\dfrac{P_1 - P_2}{P_1 + P_2}}$$

$$e = -\frac{Q_1 - Q_2}{Q_1 + Q_2} \times \frac{P_1 + P_2}{P_1 - P_2}$$

where $(2,5) = (P_1, Q_1)$ and $(4,3) = (P_2, Q_2)$ so that

$$e = \left(\frac{5 - 3}{5 + 3} \times \frac{2 + 4}{2 - 4} \right)$$

or
$$e = -\left(\frac{2}{8} \times \frac{6}{-2}\right)$$

$$= -\left(\frac{-3}{4}\right) = \frac{3}{4}$$

Notice that by using the midpoint formula, we have computed the elasticity at a point halfway between (2,5) and (4,3). This point is (3,4), because the demand curve is a straight line.

Let us now evaluate the elasticity at (3,4) by finding the point elasticity. To do this, we must return to our original definition of elasticity, where it was said that $e = \frac{\Delta Q}{\Delta P} \times \frac{P}{Q}$. Now, if we are only dealing with one point, we can't very well evaluate Δ_Q and Δ_P. Therefore we must imagine starting out with an arc elasticity and letting Δ_P become very small. As $\Delta_P \to 0$, calculus tells us that $\frac{\Delta Q}{\Delta P} \to \frac{DQ}{DP}$, so that for point elasticity, $e = \frac{DQ}{DP} \times \frac{P}{Q}$. Notice that this is simply the reciprocal of the slope multiplied by a factor of P/Q. At the point (3,4), $P/Q = 3/4$ and since demand is given by the formula $Q = 7 - P$, $DQ/DP = -1$. Then $e = \frac{DQ}{DP} \times \frac{P}{Q} = (-1)\left(\frac{3}{4}\right) = -\frac{3}{4}$. Dropping the minus sign, we once again have e = 3/4 at point $(P,Q) = (3,4)$

A simple diagram clarifies the issue. First we draw a non-linear demand curve *DD*, and then the linear demand curve *D'D'*. Suppose the

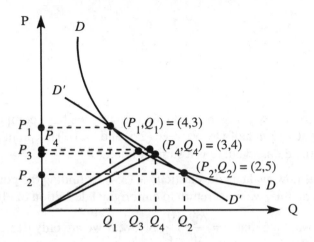

slope of the non-linear demand curve at point (P_3,Q_3) equals the slope of the linear demand curve, i.e., the line tangent at DD in point (P_3,Q_3) is parallel to D'D', say $\dfrac{\Delta Q_3}{\Delta P_3}$. Then the point-elasticity in point (P_3,Q_4)

is $e_3 = \dfrac{\frac{\Delta Q_3}{Q_3}}{\frac{\Delta P_3}{P_3}} = \dfrac{\Delta Q_3}{\Delta P_3} \cdot \dfrac{P_3}{Q_3}$, and in point (P_4,Q_4) is $e_4 = \dfrac{\frac{\Delta Q_4}{Q_4}}{\frac{\Delta P_4}{P_4}} = \dfrac{\Delta Q_4}{\Delta P_4} \cdot \dfrac{P_4}{Q_4}$

But we stated that $\dfrac{\Delta Q_3}{\Delta P_3} = \dfrac{\Delta Q_4}{\Delta P_4}$; substituting in gives us $e_3 = \dfrac{\Delta Q_4}{\Delta P_4} \cdot \dfrac{P_3}{Q_3}$

and we see that the point elasticities in (P_3,Q_3) and (P_4,Q_3) are in general not equal. The arc elasticity measured over the arc from (P_1,Q_1) to (P_2,Q_2), equals the point elasticity of (P_3,Q_4), but not of point (P_4,Q_3).

1.9.3 The Geometric Computation of Elasticity

Horizontal Axis Formula

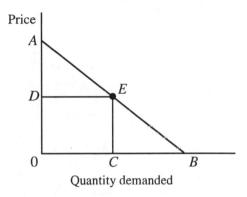

Price elasticity of demand at point E on demand curve AB is:

$$\eta = \left[\frac{\Delta Q}{\Delta P} \cdot \frac{P}{Q}\right] = \left[\frac{CB}{CE} \cdot \frac{CE}{OC}\right] = \frac{CB}{OC}$$

Vertical Axis Formula (using the same diagram)

$$\eta = \left[\frac{\Delta Q}{\Delta P} \cdot \frac{P}{Q}\right] = \left[\frac{DE}{DA} \cdot \frac{OD}{DE}\right] = \frac{OD}{DA}$$

1.9.4 Five Categories of η

Effects on Expenditures:

1. $|\eta| = 0$ **perfectly inelastic** $\uparrow p, \overline{q_b} \to \uparrow$ expenditure

2. $|\eta| < 1$ **inelastic** $\uparrow p > \downarrow q_D \to \uparrow$ expenditure

3. $|\eta| = 1$ **unitary elastic** $\uparrow p = \downarrow q_D \rightarrow$ expenditure
constant

4. $|\eta| > 1$ **elastic** $\uparrow p < \downarrow q_D \rightarrow \downarrow$ expenditure

5. $|\eta| = \infty$ **perfectly elastic**   A very small ΔP causes the Q_d
to become 0 or ∞, depending on
the direction of the price change.

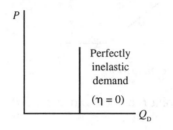

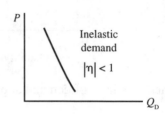

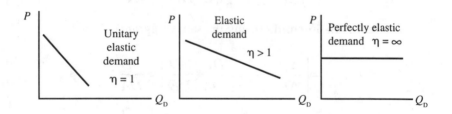

Problem Solving Example:

 Define elasticity of demand.

Elasticity of demand is a term widely used in economics to indicate the degree of responsiveness, or sensitiveness, of the quantity demanded attributable to a given change in an independent variable such as the price of X, prices of competitive goods, expectations of price changes, consumer incomes, tastes and preferences, or advertising expenditures. Let us discuss the price-elasticity of demand. Elasticity ends up qualitatively in one of three alternative categories.

1. Unitary elasticity where $|\varepsilon p| = 1.0$. This is the situation where the percentage change in quantity demanded divided by the percentage change in price equals 1. Since price and quantity are inversely related, this means that the effect on revenues of a price change is exactly offset by a change in quantity demanded, with the result that total revenue, the product of $P \times Q$ or (Price × Quantity), remains constant.

2. Elastic demand (that is, $|\varepsilon p| > 1.0$), results when the relative change in quantity demanded is larger than that in price. So a given percentage increment in price causes demand to decrease by a larger percentage, resulting in a decrease in total revenue. Thus, if demand is elastic, a price increase will lower total revenue, and a decrease will raise total revenue.

Example: $\varepsilon p = +3.0$

3. Inelastic demand, $|\varepsilon p| < 1.0$, occurs when a price increase will produce a less than proportionate decrease in quantity demanded so that total revenues will rise.

Example: $\varepsilon p = +0.5$

The equation for calculating any elasticity is

$$\text{Elasticity} = \frac{\text{Percentage Change in } Q}{\text{Percentage Change in } X}$$

$$= \frac{\Delta Q}{\dfrac{(Q_1 + Q_2)}{2}} \div \frac{\Delta P}{\dfrac{(P_1 + P_2)}{2}}.$$

Dividing by a ratio is equal to multiplying by its inverse, thus

$$\varepsilon_p = \frac{\Delta Q}{\Delta P} \cdot \frac{\dfrac{(P_1 + P_2)}{2}}{\dfrac{(Q_1 + Q_2)}{2}}$$

and

$$\varepsilon_p = \frac{\Delta Q}{\Delta P} \cdot \frac{(P_1 + P_2)}{2} \cdot \frac{2}{(Q_1 + Q_2)},$$

so

$$\varepsilon_p = \frac{\Delta Q}{\Delta P} \cdot \frac{(P_1 + P_2)}{(Q_1 + Q_2)}$$

Where Q is quantity demanded, P is the independent variable, i.e., in the discussion, the price, and Δ designates the amount of change in a variable.

1.9.5 Determinants of η

Elastic =
luxuries
many substitutes
large part of budget
longer time period
large number of product uses

Inelastic =
necessities
few substitutes
small part of budget
shorter time period
small number of product uses

Total Revenue Test—determines η

total revenue = price × quantity = $f(\eta)$

inelastic D $\qquad \downarrow P \rightarrow \downarrow TR$

elastic D $\qquad \downarrow P \rightarrow \uparrow TR$

unitary elastic D $\qquad \downarrow P \rightarrow \overline{TR}$

Thus, looking at total revenue is an easy way to determine the characteristics of elasticity.

Linear Constant Slope Case:

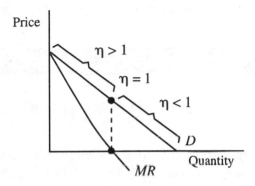

Figure 1.13 Constant Slope Demand Case

Note: Along a straight line demand curve, slope is constant, but elasticity changes because slope is an absolute measure and elasticity is a relative measure.

$$MR \text{ (marginal revenue)} = \text{rate of change of } TR; MR = \frac{\Delta TR}{\Delta Q}$$

$\eta - 1$ at the exact midpoint of the demand curve.
When $MR = 0$, TR is max $= 1$ and η is unitary elastic.
When $MR < 0$, η is inelastic.
When $MR > 0$, η is elastic.

1.9.6 Cross Elasticity of Demand ($\eta_{A, B}$)

Substitutes $= \eta_{\text{good } A, \text{ good } B} > 0$

Complements $= \eta_{\text{good } A, \text{ good } B} < 0$

$$\eta_{\text{good } A, \text{ good } B} = \frac{\Delta Q_A}{Q_A} \div \frac{\Delta P_B}{P_B}$$

The cross elasticity of demand is the relation between the percent change in q_D of one good and the percent change in price of another good.

Problem Solving Example:

 What is meant by cross elasticity of demand?

Cross elasticity is the ratio between the percentage change in the quantity demanded of a good and the percentage change in the price of another good. Like all elasticity formulas, it takes the general form of the expression for elasticity of demand. Specifically,

$$e_{A,B} = \frac{\dfrac{\Delta Q_A}{Q_A}}{\dfrac{\Delta P_B}{P_B}}$$

where $e_{A,B}$ = cross elasticity of demand for product A with respect to the price of product B

Q_A	=	quantity of product A
ΔQ_A	=	change in quantity of product A
P_B	=	price of product B
ΔP_B	=	change in price of product B

If the cross elasticity of demand is positive, then an increase in the price of product B will increase the quantity demanded of product A; products A and B are substitutes. If the cross elasticity of demand is negative, then an increase in the price of product B will cause the quantity demanded of product A to fall; products A and B are complements.

1.9.7   Income Elasticity of Demand (μ)

The income elasticity of demand is the responsiveness of quantity demanded of an item to changes in income.

$$\mu = \frac{\%\Delta q_D}{\%\Delta Y} = \frac{\Delta q_D}{\Delta q_d} \div \frac{\Delta Y}{Y}$$

Categories of μ

1. μ > 0   superior/normal goods $\uparrow Y \rightarrow \uparrow$ expenditure

2. μ < 0   inferior/poor man's
   goods $\uparrow Y \rightarrow \downarrow$ expenditure

3. μ > 1   luxuries $\uparrow Y \rightarrow \uparrow$ expenditure $> \uparrow Y$

4. μ < 1   necessities $\uparrow Y \rightarrow \uparrow$ expenditure $< \uparrow Y$

Note: These different types of goods will be explained in Chapter 2.

Problem Solving Example:

Q What is meant by income elasticity of demand?

A Income elasticity of demand is defined as the percentage change in quantity of a good demanded divided by the percentage change in a consumer's income. The difference between this elasticity and price elasticity of demand is that income has taken the place of price in the role of independent variable. Mathematically, the concept can be expressed as follows:

$$e_y = \frac{\dfrac{\Delta q}{q}}{\dfrac{\Delta Y}{Y}}$$

where e_y = Income elasticity of demand

           q = quantity demand

and   Y = income.

Suppose that $e_y > 0$ for product A. Then as income increases, you spend more of your income on product A than you did before the increase. Such products are called superior, or normal, goods. Examples of normal goods would be shoes and steaks. If $e_I < 0$ for product B, then you spend less on product B after an increase in income than you spent before the increase. Such products are called inferior, or "poor man's," goods. An example of this would be the potato. If you are very poor, you might have to eat a lot of potatoes because they are relatively inexpensive. However, as income rises, you would find yourself able to purchase meats and vegetables that are more expensive than potatoes, but at least bring some variety to your menu. Consequently, as income increases, your potato consumption will most likely fall.

A further break-up of income elasticities is also used. Specifically, if $e_y > 1$, income elasticity of demand is said to be high and goods of such elasticity are considered luxuries. Remember that if $e_y > 1$ for product c, this means that as income increases, not only does your absolute consumption of product c increase, but also the percentage of income spent on product c is increasing. Suppose you are making $2,000 per year and can afford steak once a year. If your income increases to $20,000, you can now afford steak every week. Here is an example of elasticity greater than 1. However, the reader should be careful not to assume that $e_y > 1$ over all income ranges. Suppose income now rose from $20,000 to $200,000. Surely, you could now afford steak every night and if e_y were greater than 1, you would eat steak every night. Yet you won't because you would get sick of steak eventually. Therefore we must remember that income elasticities often vary and must be defined over a range of income.

Those goods that have $e_y < 1$ are considered necessities.

1.9.8 Elasticity of Supply

$$\varepsilon = \frac{\%\Delta q_s}{\%\Delta P} = \frac{\Delta q_D}{\Delta q_s} \div \frac{\Delta P}{P}$$

Categories of ε

1. $\varepsilon = 0$ perfectly inelastic
2. $\varepsilon < 1$ inelastic
3. $\varepsilon = 1$ unitary elastic
4. $\varepsilon > 1$ elastic
5. $\varepsilon = \infty$ perfectly elastic, the "constant cost" case

Linear/Constant Slope Supply Case

Linear supply curve $= \varepsilon > 1$ if cuts P axis

$\varepsilon = 1$ if passes through origin

$\varepsilon < 1$ if cuts Q axis

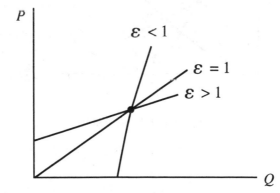

Figure 1.14

Marshall's Three Time Periods:

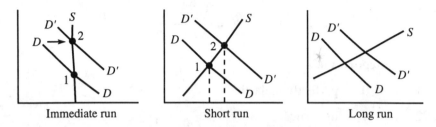

| Immediate run | Short run | Long run |

Figure 1.15

Note: Effects of ΔD over time: elasticity of supply increases in the long run because there is more time for adjustments to the changes in prices. The immediate run implies a fixed supply.

Effects of Shifts of S, $D = f\,(\eta, \varepsilon) =$

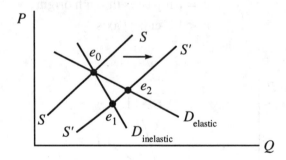

Figure 1.16 Supply shift

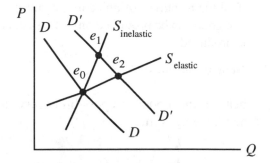

Figure 1.17 Demand Shift

Quiz: Fundamentals of Supply and Demand

1. The basic difference between consumer goods and capital goods is that

    (A) consumer goods are produced in the private sector and investment goods are produced in the public sector.

    (B) an economy that commits a relatively large proportion of its resources to capital goods must accept a lower growth rate.

    (C) consumer goods satisfy wants directly, while capital goods satisfy wants indirectly.

    (D) None of the above.

2. The production possibility (or transformation) curve illustrates the basic principle that

    (A) an economy will automatically seek that level of output at which all of its resources are employed.

    (B) an economy's capacity to produce increases in proportion to its population size.

(C) if all the resources of an economy are in use, more of one good can be produced only if less of another good is produced.

(D) None of the above.

3. The figure below is the production possibility curve for nation X. Which of the following is true?

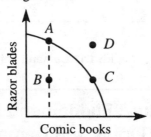

(A) Nation X cannot move from point *A* to point *C* without an increase in technology or the amount of resources used.

(B) Nation X can move from point *B* to point *C* with no increase in technology or the amount of resources used.

(C) Nation X can move from point *D* to point *A* if it ceases to produce razor blades.

(D) At point *B*, nation X can produce either more razor blades or more comic books, but not more of each.

(E) If nation X is at point *C* and decides to produce 10 less comic books, point *B* must result.

4. According to the Law of Diminishing Returns, as each additional fisherman is added to the crew of a boat, the additional amount of fish caught will

(A) increase steadily.

(B) decrease steadily.

(C) decrease, then increase.

(D) eventually decrease.

(E) fluctuate wildly.

5.   Assume that the demand for product *A* is downward sloping. If the price of *A* falls from $3.00 to $2.75,

(A) the demand for *A* will fall.

(B) the demand for *A* will rise.

(C) the quantity demanded of *A* will fall.

(D) the quantity demanded of *A* will rise.

(E) the quantity demanded of *A* won't change.

6.   If the demand curve for product *B* shifts to the right as the price of product *A* declines, it can be concluded that

(A) *A* and *B* are substitutes.

(B) *A* and *B* are complementary goods.

(C) *A* is an inferior good and *B* is a superior good.

(D) *A* is a superior good and *B* is an inferior good.

(E) both *A* and *B* are inferior goods.

7.   An equilibrium price occurs when

(A) *P* is set equal to *Q*.

(B) there is a shortage and no surplus.

(C) quantity supplied is equal to quantity demanded.

(D) All of the above.

8.   Price ceilings and price floors

(A) shift supply and demand curves and, therefore, have no effect on the rationing of prices.

    (B)   clear the market.

    (C)   always result in shortages.

    (D)   interfere with the rationing function of prices.

9.   The elasticity coefficient of demand indicates

    (A)   the slope of the demand function.

    (B)   the degree of concentration in the market.

    (C)   the extent to which a demand curve shifts as income changes.

    (D)   consumer responsiveness to price changes.

10.   Suppose the supply of product A is perfectly elastic. If there is an increase in demand for this product,

    (A)   equilibrium price and quantity will both increase.

    (B)   equilibrium price and quantity will both decrease.

    (C)   equilibrium quantity will increase but price will not change.

    (D)   equilibrium price will increase but quantity will not change.

ANSWER KEY

1.	(C)	6.	(B)
2.	(C)	7.	(C)
3.	(B)	8.	(D)
4.	(D)	9.	(D)
5.	(D)	10.	(C)

CHAPTER 2

Consumer Theory

2.1 Consumer Preferences

Consumer Sovereignty, as espoused by Adam Smith: Consumption is the sole purpose of production. Therefore, it is the foundation of the economic system. A consumer can register his preferences in the marketplace by his dollar vote. (**Note:** This premise is limited by imperfect competition, income distribution, and business-created demand.)

Assumptions Concerning Consumer Behavior:

1. **Rationality**—consumers are rational.

2. **Preferences**—preferences exist over various goods in the market (i.e., knowledge of marginal utilities).

3. **Budget Constraint**—budget/income (Y) is limited in its amount.

4. **Price**—exists due to scarcity of resources and unlimited wants.

Problem Solving Example:

 What is meant by "consumer sovereignty"?

Consumer sovereignty refers to the role of consumers in determining the types and quantities of goods produced. Consumers spend the incomes from the sale of their resources on the goods that they desire most urgently. These consumer expenditures are sometimes called "dollar votes" to emphasize the fact they reflect consumer preferences among products in the market. If there are enough "dollar votes" for a product to provide a profit to its producers, they will produce the good. An increase in "dollar votes" for a good (an increase in demand) will lead to higher prices for the good and higher profits for its producers, and hence, an expansion of the industry as producers attempt to capture the higher profits to be made in the industry. A decrease in demand will result in lower prices and lower profits, and an eventual contraction of the industry as producers seek higher profits in other industries. So changes in consumer demand for various products generate corresponding changes in the supply of those products.

Thus, in the capitalist system, consumers ultimately determine the types and quantities of goods that profit-seeking businesses will produce. This important role of consumer preferences in capitalism is characterized as "consumer sovereignty."

2.2 Cardinal Approach = Measurable Utility

2.2.1 Preference Comparison Types

Cardinal (1, 2, 3, ...)—Speaks of concrete quantities when describing preferences; "*A* is <u>twice</u> as good as *B*."

Ordinal (1st, 2nd, 3rd, ...)—Ranks in order of preference but does not say anything about any absolute measurable difference between them.

Problem Solving Example:

 Differentiate between the cardinal approach and the ordinal approach to the study of consumer demand theory.

Cardinal numbers are those that assign a concrete quantity, such as 1, 2, 3, and 4. These numbers say that 2 is twice as great as 1 and that the absolute difference between them is 1. On the other hand, ordinal numbers are those that establish a rank or order among the things to which they have been assigned, such as first, second, and third. These numbers do not say anything about the absolute difference or any other relationship between them, other than "first" is greater than "second" if we are viewing the numbers in descending order.

The classical approach to the study of consumer demand theory is generally called the cardinal utility approach. It involves the use of marginal utility and as such requires the measurement of satisfaction in absolute terms. The ordinal approach to the study of consumer demand theory, on the other hand, uses indifference analysis, relying only on a ranking of preferences for various goods.

2.2.2 The Classical Approach

The Classical Approach to Consumer Demand Theory is a cardinal approach. It uses the concept of marginal utility and thus requires measurability of taste and preferences in the absolute terms.

2.2.3 Utility

Utility (Total Utility = TU)—Power of satisfaction or happiness from a want. Utility is a subjective notion. Utility (U) for a good varies between individuals; thus, no precise quantitative measurement exists (hence, the division between Classical and Ordinal Approaches). The Classical Approach uses the term "utils" as a measurement of utility.

Note: Utility $\neq$ usefulness.

Marginal Utility (MU) = rate of change in *TU*. Marginal utility is defined as the change in total utility.

Problem Solving Example:

 What is utility? What is marginal utility?

Utility is the power to satisfy a want. When one is thirsty, water has utility, i.e., it is able to quench one's thirst. If a person prefers a strawberry sundae to hot fudge, it is said that the utility, or want-satisfying power, to that person of a strawberry sundae is greater than that of hot fudge.

"Utility" and "usefulness" need not be synonymous. Pet rocks may be "useless" yet be of tremendous utility to Christmas shoppers who can't think of what to buy their friend "who has everything."

Also, utility is a subjective notion. The utility of a specific product will vary widely from person to person. That first cigarette upon waking up in the morning will yield a great deal of utility to the chain smoker, but would have little or negative utility for someone who doesn't smoke.

Marginal utility is the extra utility, or satisfaction, that a consumer derives from an additional unit of a specific good.

2.2.4 *TU, MU* Curves

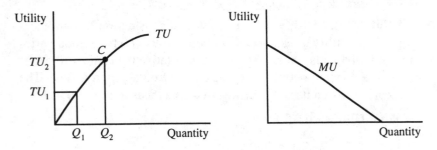

Figure 2.1

MU is the slope of the *TU* curve at the given point *C*.

↑ Consumption of a good ⇒ ↑*TU*, ↓*MU*

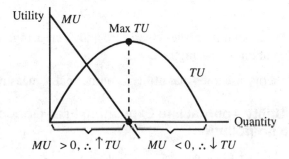

Figure 2.2

TU Curve:

The *TU* curve usually has an upside down "U" shape due to the Law of Diminishing Marginal Utility.

TU Shape:

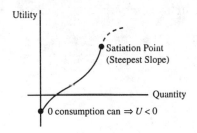

Figure 2.3

–Not normal if there is no satiation point; usually utility is not "ever-increasing" (i.e., Au miser = more have, more want).

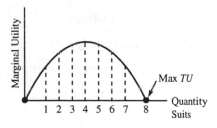

Figure 2.4

–Max *TU* at eight suits (carefully look at labeling of axes)

1. When *MU* is greater than zero and decreasing, total utility is growing at a decreasing rate.

2. When marginal utility is equal to zero, total utility is at the maximum.

3. When marginal utility is less than zero and decreasing, total utility is falling at an increasing rate.

Note: *MU* theory assumes that utility is numerically measurable.

Marginal Utility Approach to Explaining Free Goods (i.e., air, assuming no pollution):

Q_{air} available > Q air needed; therefore, its $MU = 0$.

Note: Air has a very high total utility which has no bearing on its price.

Problem Solving Example:

 Suppose marginal (MU) and total utility (TU) look as graphed in the accompanying figure.

a) Explain the shape of the *TU* curve up to point *M*.

b) What is happening at point *A*?

c) Explain the *TU* curve after point *M*.

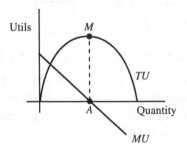

A a) Total utility curves typically, as in the figure are shaped like upside-down U's. The reason for this is the law of diminishing marginal utility. We start at Q = 0. The first unit of the product brings about a certain level of satisfaction (utils) but all units after the first bring less and less satisfaction. This is also illustrated by the shape of the *MU* curve. As more and more units of the product are consumed, *MU* grows smaller and smaller, hence the negative slope.

To explain the U-shape of the total utility curve, we say that, at first, it is increasing at a decreasing rate. *MU* is the rate of change of *TU*. As long as *MU* > 0, *TU* is increasing. But since *MU* is getting smaller, *TU* is increasing, but at a slower and slower rate. Hence, the levelling off of the *TU* curve appears.

b) At point *A*, *MU* = 0. Also when quantity = *A*, *TU* is at a maximum. These two concepts go hand-in-hand. To the left of *A*, *MU* > 0. Therefore to the left of *M*, *TU* is increasing. To the right of *A*, *MU* < 0. Therefore, to the right of *M*, *TU* is decreasing. If *TU* is increasing as it approaches *M* and decreasing as it goes away from *M*, it must reach a maximum at *M*.

c) After point *M*, *TU* is decreasing. Here the consumer has reached maximum satisfaction. More consumption of the product can only bring about dissatisfaction. (It's like eating too much of a good thing. After a while, your stomach starts to hurt). This is represented by the shape of the *MU* curve. Since *MU* < 0 after point *A*, this means that the change in *TU* is negative, i.e., *TU* is decreasing. Since *MU* itself is becoming more and more negative, *TU* will fall at a quicker and quicker pace. Thus the upside-down U-shape is explained.

2.2.5 Utility Maximization

The goal of consumers is to spend their income in a way that allows them to obtain the greatest possible satisfaction, or total utility, for their limited means or income for the present and the future.

Problem Solving Example:

 What is the utility-maximizing rule?

In dealing with the behavior of the so-called "rational" consumer, economists assume that he attempts to dispose of his money income in such a way as to derive the greatest amount of satisfaction, or total utility, from it. The consumer's goal is assumed to be utility maximization. In making his choices of goods and services, the typical consumer has a limited number of dollars in his pocket and the products he wants have price tags on them. Therefore he will be able to purchase only a limited amount of goods.

Since his purchases are limited by his budget, the consumer must decide which specific collection of goods and services will yield the greatest amount of satisfaction. To do this, the rational consumer uses the utility maximizing rule which prescribes the allocation of money income in such a way that the last dollar spent on each product purchased yields the same amount of extra (marginal) utility. To help explain this rule, let us examine an illustration. Suppose Mr. X is trying to decide which combination of good A and B he should buy with his limited budget of $10. Assume product A costs $1 and product B costs $2. The table provides utility data necessary for solving. Notice how diminishing marginal utility sets in.

(1)	(2) Product A: price = $1		(3) Product B: price = $2	
Unit of product	(a) Marginal utility, utils	(b) Marginal utility per dollar (MU / price)	(a) Marginal utility, utils	(b) Marginal utility per dollar (MU / price)
First	10	10	24	12
Second	8	8	20	10
Third	7	7	18	9
Fourth	6	6	16	8
Fifth	5	5	12	6
Sixth	4	4	6	3
Seventh	3	3	4	2

In columns 2a and 3a, we see the marginal utility of products A and B measured in utils. We must also construct columns 2b and 3b where we have marginal utility (MU) per dollar = MU/price. The point is this: to make the amounts of extra utility derived from differently priced goods comparable, marginal utility must be put on a per-dollar-spent basis, as is done in columns 2b and 3b.

Now that we have Mr. X's marginal utility data, it must be decided in what order he should allocate his dollars on units of A and B to achieve the highest degree of utility. Concentrating on columns 2b and 3b, we see that Mr. X should first purchase one unit of B since it yields the greatest utility. This costs $2 and leaves $8 to spend. Next, Mr. X is indifferent about buying A or B since they both yield ten utils. Suppose he buys both of them; Mr. X now has 1 unit of A and 2 units of B and $5 left. Note that with this combination of goods, the last dollar spent on each yields the same amount of extra utility. But Mr. X keeps going since he has $5 more.

Since the third unit of B yields 9 utils, Mr. X will choose that, leaving him with $3. Then finally, Mr. X will purchase one more unit of A and B each since the second unit of A and the fourth unit of B each yield 8 utils. This leaves Mr. X without any money, so, to maximize utility, Mr. X will purchase four units of B and two units of A with total utility equaling $10 + 8 + 24 + 20 + 18 + 16 = 96$ utils. If the reader examines some of the other possible combinations of A and B, it will become apparent that A = 2 and B = 4 is the optimal combination. Looking at columns 2a and 3a, we see that trading off the fourth unit of B for the third and fourth unit of A would be giving up 16 utils for $7 + 6 = 13$ utils in return.

Alternatively, giving up the original two units of A for a fifth unit of B would give up 18 utils for 12 utils in return. Once again, a loss in total utility would take place. So A = 2 and B = 4 represent the point of utility maximization.

2.3 Law of Diminishing Marginal Utility

The Law of Diminishing Marginal Utility says that marginal utility decreases as a consumer acquires more and more units of a certain good. This helps explain how a consumer's income is allocated among commodities and time periods. Increased consumption of a good results in greater total utility, but the utility grows at a slower rate because with each extra unit, the consumer's appreciation for that good lessens. This law explains the slopes of the total and marginal utility curves. It also explains the fact that discount prices are often contingent on the purchase of extra quantities of a good.

2.3.1 Law of Demand

If successive units of a good provide less and less marginal utility, the amount a consumer will pay for these extra units will also decrease; hence, the slope of the demand curve is negative. Normally, only by lowering a price of a good can the consumer be induced to buy more of that good.

Problem Solving Example:

 What is the Law of Demand?

The Law of Demand states that the quantity of a good demanded by an individual or group is greater (less) the lower (higher) the per unit price of the good, other things being equal. Alternatively expressed, it states that the maximum per unit price at which an individual or group member is willing and able to buy a given quantity of a good is greater (less) the smaller (larger) the quantity of that good, other factors remaining the same.

The Law of Demand, then, asserts that there is an "inverse" or "negative" relationship between the price of a good and the quantity of it demanded by an individual or group. That is, as one variable increases, the other decreases.

2.3.2   Using the Law of Diminishing *MU* to Justify Progressive Income Taxes

The argument here is that the sacrifice of the rich is less than the sacrifice of the poor for a given reduction in real income.

Problem Solving Example:

Q How is the theory of Diminishing Marginal Utility used to justify the "progressive" income tax? What is the weakness of the argument?

A The Theory of Diminishing Marginal Utility states that each additional unit of a good or service results in less-and-less added satisfaction for an individual. It is the Theory of Diminishing Marginal Utility which helps account for the downward slope of a demand curve.

Under a progressive tax system, a higher proportion of income goes to taxes as income increases. For example, an income of $20,000 might be taxed at 25%, while an income of $30,000 might be taxed at 30%.

The whole idea of progressive taxes can be seen as an extension of the Theory of Diminishing Marginal Utility, where we examine the marginal utility of an individual's income. When applied to a progressive tax system, the theory says that those people with high incomes are sacrificing less when they are asked to pay X dollars in the tax than poor people would sacrifice to pay that same amount, since the utility derived by the relatively rich from an additional X dollars is lower than that derived by the relatively poor due to their respective utility positions. For example, a poor family might have to go without some of the necessities of life to meet a $100 tax bill, but a rich family would simply have to give up some luxuries for a few days.

The weakness of the argument stems from the fact that it overlooks the subjective nature of utility. That is, while a given individual can compare the utilities to him or her of different goods, the utility that a given good has for two different individuals cannot be compared. There is no basis in economics for the claim that the marginal utility of a dollar is less to a wealthy person than to a poor person, since utility is subjective. Interpersonal comparisons of utility would require that utility be something objective.

2.4 Indifference Curves (IC)

Indifference Curves are smooth graphs representing combinations of two goods such that an individual is indifferent as to which combination he/she receives because they yield equal levels of satisfaction. In our study of marginal utility in the previous section, we assumed that utility was measured in the cardinal sense. In this section, we measure utility in the ordinal sense. We know if a bundle is preferred to another, but we cannot see by how much it is preferred.

2.4.1 Properties of Indifference Curves

1. Indifference curves are negatively sloped (slope downward and to the right).

2. There exist an infinite number of indifference curves in the commodity space. That is, indifference curves are everywhere dense.

3. Indifference curves can never intersect.

4. Along any indifference curve the utility is constant.

5. Indifference curves are generally convex to the origin.

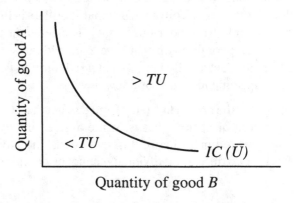

Quantity of good B

Figure 2.5 An Indifference Curve

Note: Precise shape/slope of IC varies between individuals. The slope of the IC measures the relative marginal utilities of the goods.

Problem Solving Example:

 What is indifference analysis? What is an indifference curve?

Indifference analysis is a consumer behavior theory which expresses the consumer's tastes by using curves (indifference curves) that show his or her preferences among various combinations of goods. It is a different approach to consumer behavior from cardinal utility analysis, which relies on the measurability of tastes and preferences. Indifference analysis relies only on the ability to rank goods in order of preference. For example, cardinal marginal utility analysis assumes that a consumer is able to express his tastes for products A and B by assigning a specific number of "utils" to each. Thus, he may indicate that he likes A twice as much as he likes B. Indifference analysis, on the other hand, only asks the consumer to rank his preferences — to say whether he likes A more than B, B more than A, or is indifferent between them.

An indifference curve is a smooth graph which represents the various combinations of two goods that an individual would wish to consume in order to attain a constant given level of satisfaction. That is to say, a person is "indifferent" as to whether he consumes one or another combination of goods on the same indifference curve.

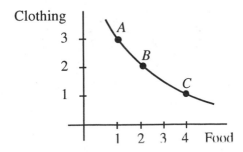

This figure represents a typical indifference curve. At point A, our consumer has three units of clothing and one unit of food. At B, he has two units of clothing and two units of food. At C, he has one unit of clothing and four units of food. Given the choice among A, B, and C, our consumer would be indifferent, since each of these three points yields exactly the same level of satisfaction.

2.5 Marginal Rate of Substitution and Law of Substitution

2.5.1 Marginal Rate of Substitution (MRS)

The MRS is the amount of one good that an individual is willing to give up in order to get one more unit of another good and still remain on the same indifference curve.

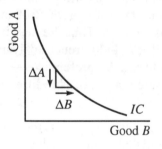

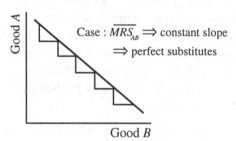

Case : $\overrightarrow{MRS_{AB}} \Rightarrow$ constant slope
$\Rightarrow$ perfect substitutes

| Figure 2.6 | Figure 2.7 |

The MRS is the measurement of the slope of an indifference curve at a particular point on that indifference curve.

$$MRS_{AB} = \left| \frac{\Delta A}{\Delta B} \right| : \text{ Marginal rate of substitution of } A \text{ for } B$$

$$= \frac{MU_A}{MU_B}$$

Problem Solving Example:

Q Suppose that at a given level of satisfaction the marginal rate of substitution of product *B* for product *A* is constant. What does this imply about the relevant indifference curve?

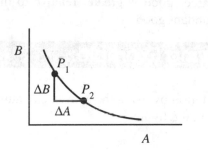 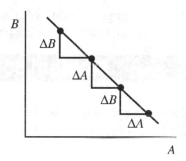

A The marginal rate of substitution of *B* for *A*, MRS_{BA}, is defined as the amount of *B* the consumer is just willing to give up in order to get one additional unit of *A* and maintain the same level of satisfaction.

On the indifference curve in the figure on the left, $MRS_{BA} = \Delta B/\Delta A$, which is a slope concept. Therefore, if $\Delta B/\Delta A$ is constant, the indifference curve is a downward-sloping straight line.

When two products present a straight line indifference curve, they are perfect substitutes.

2.5.2   Law of Substitution

The scarcer a good, the greater its relative substitution value.

1. The willingness to substitute *A* for *B* is a function of the amounts of *A* and *B* you have originally. The less units of *A* you have, the more *B* that must be given in exchange before you will be willing to give up one unit of *A*, if utility is to be kept constant.

2. The marginal utility of a scarcer good is greater relative to the marginal utility of a more abundant good.

Problem Solving Example:

 Explain the law of substitution by using the convex curvature of the indifference curve in the figure.

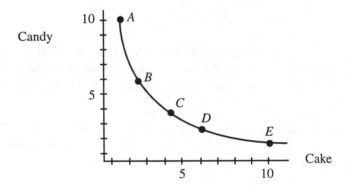

The law of substitution states that the scarcer a good is, the greater its relative substitution value, i.e., its marginal utility rises relative to the marginal utility of the good that has become relatively more plentiful.

Examining the curve in this figure, notice that as we move along the convex curve from points *A* to *E*, the slope of the curve grows more and more horizontal. In going from point *A* to point *B*, our consumer is giving up 4 units of candy for 1 unit of cake while maintaining constant utility. From point *B* to point *C*, the consumer will give up only 2 units of candy for one unit of cake. We can see that farther down the curve, candy is becoming relatively scarcer to him and cake relatively more abundant, i.e., the marginal utility of candy is rising as he gives up more and more to acquire cake.

Suppose our convex curve became perfectly horizontal after point *E*. Then the amount of candy necessary to maintain this utility level would never fall below one unit. In other words, no amount of cake could induce our consumer to give up any more of his candy.

In general, the law of substitution and the convex indifference curve are saying the same thing: the fewer units of product *A* you have, the more units of *B* you must be given in return in order to maintain a constant level of utility.

2.6 Indifference Map

An **Indifference Map** is a graph of a whole series of ICs, each one farther away from the origin, corresponding to increasing levels of total utility.

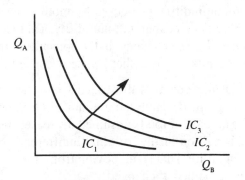

Higher ICs correspond to increase in utility.

Figure 2.8 Indifference Map

Problem Solving Examples:

The curves labeled U_1, U_2, and U_3 in the figure represent indifference curves. Describe the effects on total utility as a consumer moves from point A to points B_1, B_2, B_3, or B_4.

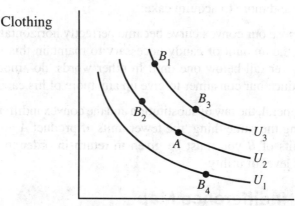

This question is asking you to describe the change in the consumer's utility level as he/she switches from point A to points B_1 through B_4 as illustrated above. If a consumer moves from one position along a single indifference curve to another position along that same curve, there is no change in total utility. That is, shifts along an indifference curve cause no change in the consumer's total satisfaction as he changes the mix of goods that he/she is consuming.

This kind of movement is illustrated when the consumer moves from point A to point B_2. Here the amount of clothing consumed increases and the amount of food consumed decreases in such a way that the consumer is still on his/her original indifference curve, the mapping of constant utility. That is, in moving from A to B_2 the consumer's total utility has remained unchanged.

As one moves in a northeasterly direction in the figure to higher indifference curves, higher and higher levels of satisfaction are represented by each new indifference curve. That is, curve U_2 stands for a higher level of satisfaction than U_1; U_3 for a higher level of satisfaction than U_2. Therefore, movements from A to B_3 (food increases, clothing increases) and from A to B_1 (food decreases, clothing increases) represent increases in total utility.

Finally, movement from curve U_2 to U_1 is southwesterly representing a move to a lower indifference curve so that this represents a decline in total utility. Going from A to B_4 (food increases, clothing decreases) represents, therefore, a drop in total utility.

 What does the indifference map illustrate?

The production indifference curves in a map constitute a complete description of the production function. For each combination of inputs, they show how much output can be produced. Each indifference curve indicates all combinations of input quantities capable of producing a given quantity of output; thus, there must be a separate indifference curve for each quantity of output.

2.7 Substitutes, Complements, and Indifference Maps

Substitutes are goods that can be used in place of another good. An example of this would be butter and margarine.

Complements are goods that must have another good to be useful. An example of this would be tennis balls and tennis rackets.

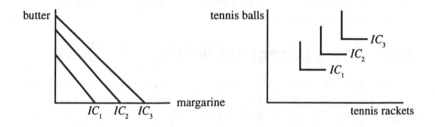

Figure 2.9 Perfect Substitutes   **Figure 2.10 Perfect Complements**

Perfect Substitutes:

1. Constant MRS along each indifference curve.

2. Corner solution, consumption of either good *A* or good *B* but not both.

Perfect Complements:

1. An increase in Q_A without an increase in Q_B does not increase the total level of utility.

2. More of both (in the same quantities) does increase the level of utility.

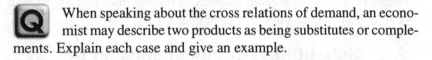

Problem Solving Example:

Q When speaking about the cross relations of demand, an economist may describe two products as being substitutes or complements. Explain each case and give an example.

A Substitutes are rival, or competing, products. That is, *A* may be used instead of *B* or vice versa. Thus, if products *A* and *B* are substitutes, a rise in the price of *A* will cause an increase in demand for *B*. An example of substitute goods would be coffee and tea.

Complements are cooperating commodities, That is, *A* will most often be used with *B*. Thus, if *A* and *B* are complements, a rise in the price of *A* will lower the demand for *B*. An example of complementary goods would be frankfurters and sauerkraut.

2.8   The Budget Line (BL)

The Budget Line or the Budget Constraint shows all obtainable combinations of two baskets of goods, given nominal income and prices of both baskets of goods. It denotes limit on expenditure, reflecting objective market data.

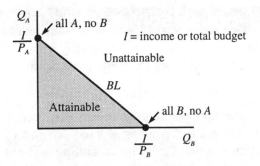

Figure 2.11 The Budget Constraint

The Budget-Line Equation

$$Q_B = \frac{\text{Budget}}{P'_B} = \frac{P_A}{P'_B} \cdot Q_A$$

2.8.1 The Slope of the Budget Constraint

The Slope of the Budget Constraint is the ratio of the prices of the two goods in question, P_B/P_A. The slope is negative, thus the price ratio is also negative.

Numerical representation of the slope is called the **Marginal Rate of Market Substitution (MRMS)** of the two goods and is the feasible rate that one can trade off A for B.

74

Consumer Theory

Problem Solving Example:

Q   What does the slope of the budget line illustrate?

A   The budget line represents all commodity combinations a consumer can get by spending a fixed amount of money. The budget line is thus a curve of constant expenditure. The slope of a Budget Line is the amount of one commodity the market requires an individual to give up in order to obtain one additional unit of another commodity without any change in the amount of money spent.

2.8.2   Location of the Budget Line

The Location of the Budget Line gives a good indication of the consumer's income. The budget line *shifts* with changes in real income or a proportional change in prices (which is a change in real income). Thus, if income grows, the budget line will shift to the right; if income falls, it will shift to the left.

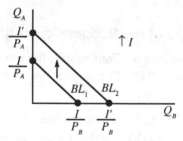

Figure 2.12 Effects of Increased Income on the Budget Line

Problem Solving Example:

Q Suppose Consumer X has $6 to spend on food and clothing, where food costs $1.50 a unit and clothing costs $1.00 a unit. Draw his consumption-possibility line.

A The consumption-possibility line, or, as it is often called, the budget line, shows the possible combinations of food and clothing which Consumer X can buy for a given amount of expenditure, in our example, $6. Let's first look at the extreme cases. X could buy all food and get $6/1.50 = 4 units. Or he could buy all clothing and get $6/1.00 = 6 units. These two possibilities represent the endpoints of the consumption-possibility line. To draw the rest of the function, draw the straight line connecting the endpoints as shown in the figure. This line is straight because clothing can be exchanged for food at a constant ratio (3 units of clothing = $6 = 2 units of food); i.e., slope = constant = -3/2.

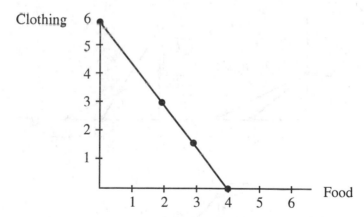

To prove to yourself that this line is really straight, note several other points on the line, including 2 units of food and 3 units of clothing or 3 units of food and $1^1/_2$ units of clothing. When plotted, these two points, as well as any other of the many possible combinations of the two goods that are affordable to the consumer, fall on a straight line.

This problem can also be approached algebraically. We have $6 to spend where each unit of food costs $1.50 and each unit of clothing costs $1. Letting x = # of units of food and y = # of units of clothing, 1.50x$ and 1.00y$ represents the total amounts spent on food and clothing, respectively. Therefore, since we have $6 to spend, the equation of the budget line is

$$\$1.50x + \$1.00y = \$6$$

or

$$\$1.50x + \$y = 6$$

$$= -\$3/2x + \$6$$

Once again, we see the budget line is a straight line with slope $= -3/2$.

2.8.3   Effects of Price Changes on the Budget Line

Changes in prices affect both the slope of the budget constraint and its location.

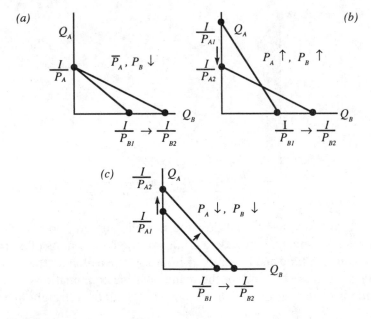

Figure 2.13 Effects of Changes in Prices on the Budget Constraint

Problem Solving Example:

 Line *AB* in the first figure represents a consumer's budget line.

a) If he has a $12 budget, what are the per-unit prices of food and clothing?
b) If the price of food falls by $1 per unit, how will *AB* shift?
c) Suppose these prices remain constant. If his budget rises to $18, how will *AB* shift?

A a) To find the per-unit prices of food and clothing, it is easiest to work with the endpoints of the line *AB*. At point *A*, no food is purchased while 4 units of clothing are purchased for $12.

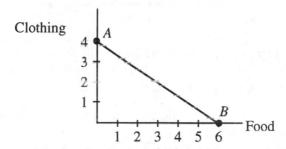

Therefore, clothing costs 12 dollars/4 units = 3 dollars per unit. At point *B*, no clothing is purchased while 6 units of food are purchased for $12. Therefore, food costs 12 dollars/6 units = 2 dollars per unit.

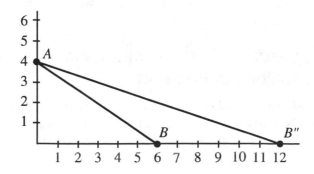

b) Now a shift in price has taken place. Specifically, the price of food has fallen from $3 to $2. This will not affect point A since the price of clothing has not changed at all. Point B, however, will shift. Whereas before a $2 price bought 6 units for $12, a $1 price will now enable a consumer to buy 12 units for $12. Therefore B will shift to B″, where food bought = 12 units as shown in the second figure.

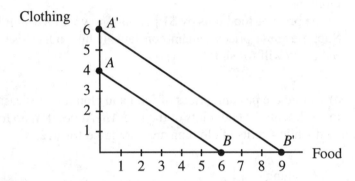

c) If this consumer's budget rises to $18, he will be able to buy more of both food and clothing than before. Therefore his budget line will shift up and to the right, as shown in the third figure.

Whereas the consumer could purchase 4 units of clothing previously at $3 per unit for $12, he can now purchase 6 units of clothing for $18. This is shown as point A′ on the graph. Also, he previously could purchase 6 units of food at $2 per unit. Now $18 buys the consumer 9 units, as shown by point B′. Then the straight line connecting A′ and B′ represents the new budget line. Notice that A′B′ is parallel to AB. As long as the prices of A and B do not change, a shift in the budget will not affect the slope of the budget line.

2.9 Consumer Maximization and Equilibrium Position

The consumer's equilibrium point and the point where the consumer maximizes his utility are the same. Let us assume that all income is being spent on only two goods, A and B. We want to choose a point on the budget line that corresponds to the highest attainable indifference curve. This can be seen in the following graph:

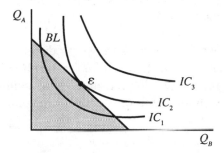

Figure 2.14 The Consumer Equilibrium Position

The highest attainable indifference curve is IC_2. The **equilibrium position**, E, occurs where IC_2 is tangent to the budget line. At this point, the consumer is at his maximum level of utility given his income; thus, he has no reason to change his consumption bundle while he is at this point. This is the consumer's equilibrium position.

2.9.1 Optimum for Consumers

Mathematically, this optimum is where the marginal rate of substitution is equal to the marginal rate of market substitution (MRMS).

$$MRS_{BA} = \frac{MU_B}{MU_A} = \frac{\Delta B}{\Delta A} = \frac{P_B}{P_A} = MRMS_{BA}$$

The Equal Marginal Principle is when:

$$\frac{MU_A}{P_A} = \frac{MU_B}{P_B}$$

This is the law of equal marginal utility per dollar for each good if maximum utility is to be attained. The last dollar spent on B must give the same level of satisfaction as the last dollar spent on A.

Problem Solving Example:

Q In indifference curve analysis, what is meant by the marginal rate of substitution?

A Suppose we are dealing with two products, A and B. Then the marginal rate of substitution of B for A, abbreviated as MRS_{BA}, is defined as the amount of B the consumer is just willing to give up in order to get one additional unit of A and still maintain the same level of satisfaction.

A	B
3	7.0
4	6.4
5	5.9
6	5.5

The table above represents various combinations of A and B where the level of satisfaction is assumed to be constant. Suppose the consumer has 3 units of A and 7.0 units of B. To get the 4th unit of A, he would give up no more than 0.6 units (7.0 – 6.4) of B. Therefore MRS_{BA} = 0.6. Then, as he acquires more A and holds less B, each unit of A becomes less important to him. Thus, he will give up a relatively small amount of B to get A as we move down the table and the MRS_{BA} falls from 0.6 to 0.5 to 0.4.

2.9.2   Hill of Happiness, Goods vs. Bads

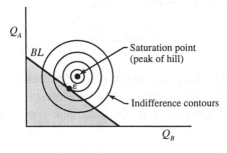

Figure 2.15 Hill of Happiness

Assumption: Individuals are rational. They want to maximize their utility and attain their highest attainable indifference curve.

Saturation Point: not often relevant due to scarcity (if the goods are free, choose saturation).

Beyond the saturation point, "goods" become "bads" (e.g., air pollution).

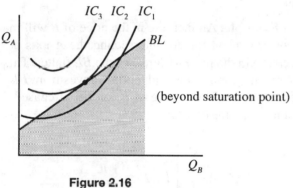

(beyond saturation point)

Figure 2.16

2.10 Effects of Changes of Income and Prices on the Consumer Equilibrium Position

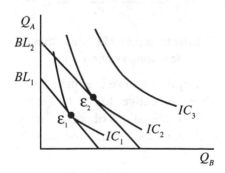

Figure 2.17 Shifts in BL on Equilibrium Position

An increase (decrease) in income or a proportional decrease (increase) in both prices will shift the BL to the right (left); the optimal choice will change to where the new *BL* is tangent to the highest attainable *IC*, where the utility derived is the greatest.

2.10.1 Single Price Changes and the Price Consumption Curve

A single price change results in a change in the slope of the budget line.

Example: An increase in the price of *B* will make the slope of *BL* steeper, leaving the *BL* intersecting the *A* axis at the same point. A decrease in the price of *B* makes the *BL* flatter. This can be seen in the following graph as the budget line moves from BL_1 to BL_4 as the price of *B* declines. Thus, more of *B* can be purchased, but not more of *A*, holding income constant.

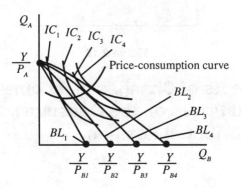

Figure 2.18 Effects of a Single Price Change and the Price Consumption Curve

The **Price-Consumption Curve** is a line drawn through the set of optimum points (where the budget line is tangent to the indifference curve) representing the combinations of good *A* and good *B* as the price of one of the goods changes and income remains constant.

2.10.2 Construction of the Demand Curve

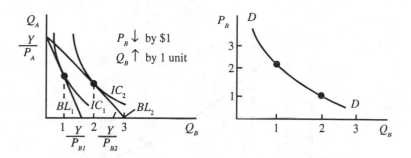

Figure 2.19 Construction of the Demand Curve

By taking the old and new equilibrium points along the price-consumption curve, one can construct the demand curve by reading-off quantities and prices corresponding to each intersection of the BL and IC curves.

Problem Solving Example:

Q Graphically, why does the demand curve, which represents all price and quantity demanded possibilities, slope downward and to the right?

A The demand curve slopes downward and to the right because there is an inverse relationship between price and the quantity demanded. The law of demand, which states that people buy more of any good at a lower price than they do at a higher price, is reflected in the downward slope of the demand curve.

Graphically, the downward sloping demand curve can be shown as in the figure.

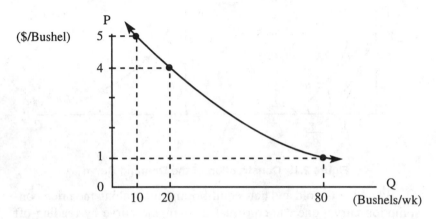

As can be seen in the figure, the quantity demanded at a price of $5 would be 10 bushels per week. If the price is reduced to $4, the quantity demanded will increase to 20 bushels. At a price of $1, people are able and willing to buy 80 bushels per week.

2.11 Income and Substitution Effects

The **Substitution Effect** occurs when a change in relative prices implies that more of the cheaper good will be purchased, holding real income constant. Because of the change in relative prices, we expect the consumer to substitute some of the cheaper good for the more expensive one.

The **Income Effect** occurs because the price change of one good causes a change in *real* income if the price of the other good and nominal income remain constant. If the price of one good falls, the consumer's real income, and hence purchasing power, will increase. Therefore, the consumer would be able to purchase more of *both* goods.

2.11.1 Hicks' Method of Isolating Income and Substitution Effects

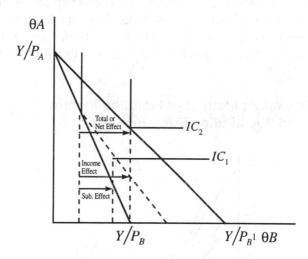

Figure 2.20 The Substitution and Income Effects – Hicks' Method

Let us assume that the consumer is initially at point X, consuming quantities A_1 and B_1, at prices P_{A1} and P_{B1}. If the price of B increases from P_{B1} to P_{B2}, the consumer's new optimum is at point Y where he is consuming quantities B_2 and A_2, where BL_2 is tangent to IC_1. He is now at a lower level of satisfaction due to the price rise of one of the goods.

To differentiate between the income and substitution effects, we must put the consumer back on his original indifference curve. To do this we move the new budget line, BL_2, parallel to itself until it reaches back to IC_2. This parallel line will reflect the new price ratio. It is given by Y_2/P_{A1}, Y_2/P_{B2}. This shift is similar to giving the consumer a subsidy

$Y_2 - Y_1$. The consumer is now at equilibrium point Z and consuming quantities A_3 and B_3.

The movement from X to Z is the substitution effect because both points have the same level of real income. If we take the subsidy away from the consumer, he moves from Z to Y. This is the income effect. So the substitution effect for good B is $B_1 - B_3$ and the income effect for good B is $B_3 - B_2$.

2.11.2 Slutsky's Method of Isolating Income and Substitution Effects

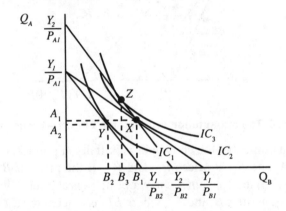

Figure 2.21 The Substitution and Income Effects – Slutsky's Method

Slutsky's Method is different from Hicks' Method in that Slutsky's does not wish to put the consumer on his original indifference curve; rather, it enables the consumer to purchase his original basket of goods before the price change. This is depicted in the graph above.

The consumer is at initial equilibrium, X, at income Y_1, and prices P_{B1} and P_{A1}. Again, let the price of good B increase to P_{B2} and let the price of good A stay the same and nominal income remain constant. However, due to the increase in the price of B, real income has fallen. The new equilibrium is again at point Y where the budget line is tangent to IC_1. To find the income and substitution effects, we again give the consumer a subsidy, but instead of giving him enough to get back to the same level of utility, we give him enough to buy the same basket of goods as he did before the price change. So we shift the budget line

parallel from $\dfrac{Y_1}{P_{A1}}, \dfrac{Y_1}{P_{B2}}$ to $\dfrac{Y_2}{P_{A1}}, \dfrac{Y_2}{P_{B2}}$, where it intersects point X.

The consumer will now consume at point Z where the new budget line,

$\dfrac{Y_2}{P_{A1}}, \dfrac{Y_2}{P_{B2}}$, is tangent to the highest attainable indifference curve, IC_3.

This, however, is now at a higher level of satisfaction than the original equilibrium point. The movement from X to Z is the substitution effect and the movement from Z to Y is the income effect when removing the subsidy given to the consumer.

2.12 Expenditure: Consumption–Income and Engel Curves

2.12.1 Consumption–Income Curve

The Consumption-Income Curve denotes changes in the choice between goods due to a change in income while prices remain constant.

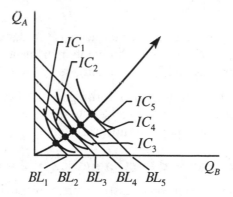

Figure 2.22 The Income-Consumption Curve

2.12.2 The Engel Curve

The Engel Curve is a line connecting the points that show different quantities of an item purchased at different levels of income.

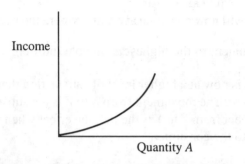

Figure 2.23 The Engel Curve

2.13 Categories of Goods: Normal, Superior, Inferior, and Giffen Goods

Normal or **Superior goods** are goods which increase in demand with an increase in income. Examples of this would be clothes, cars, vacations, etc.

Inferior goods are goods which decrease in demand as income rises. An example of this would be hamburger meat. As income increases, we might demand fewer hamburgers but more T-bone steaks.

Giffen Goods are very strong inferior goods. A fall in price results in a reduction in the quantity demanded. In the case of a Giffen Good, the demand curve has a positive (upward) slope.

2.13.1 Elasticities and the Categories of Goods

Price elasticity and income elasticity are explained in Chapter 1.

Categories of Income Elasticities (μ)

1. $\mu > 0$ superior/normal goods $\uparrow Y \rightarrow \uparrow$ expenditure

2. $\mu < 0$ inferior goods $\uparrow Y \rightarrow \downarrow$ expenditure

3. $\mu > 1$ luxuries $\uparrow Y \rightarrow \uparrow$ expenditure
                                   ($\uparrow\% \ Y$ spent)

4. $\mu < 1$ necessities $\uparrow Y \rightarrow \uparrow$ expenditure
                                   ($\downarrow\% \ Y$ spent)

2.13.2 Income and Substitution Effects and the Categories of Goods

Normal Good—As the price of a normal good declines, the quantity demanded of that good increases. Both the income and substitution effects of that good are positive. The slope of the demand curve is negative.

Inferior Goods—The substitution effect is still positive, that is, as the price declines, the quantity demanded increases, but the income effect is negative. A **Giffen Good** is an inferior good whose income effect predominates the substitution effect.

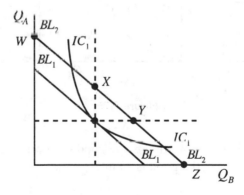

Figure 2.24 Normal and Inferior Goods

If income increases, the budget line will shift out from BL_1 to BL_2. If the new consumer's optimum lies between the points X and Y, then both goods are normal. However, if the new optimum lies between W and X, then good A is normal and good B is inferior. If the new optimum lies between Y and Z, then B is a normal good and A is an inferior good.

Problem Solving Example:

 What is meant by the terms "normal good" and "inferior good"?

 Normal goods are those whose demand curve varies directly with income. They are also called superior goods.

Inferior or "poor man's" goods are those whose demand curve shifts downward with an increase in income. For example, as people earn more, they are able to afford brand name products. This will reduce their demand for generic substitutes.

2.13.3 The Engel Curve and the Categories of Goods

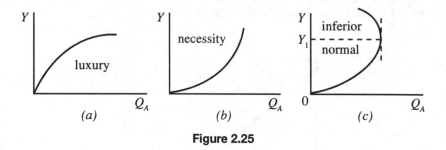

Figure 2.25

In Graph c in the above figure, the good is a normal good between 0 and Y_1, but above Y_1 the good is an inferior one.

2.14 Consumer Surplus

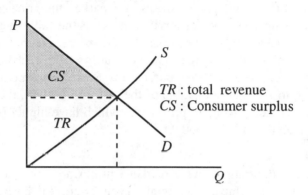

TR : total revenue
CS : Consumer surplus

Figure 2.26 Consumer Surplus

Consumer Surplus is a measure of benefit to a consumer above the actual cost to him. In a perfect market, there is one price for all homogeneous goods, $P_{all\ units} = P_{last\ unit}$. However, earlier units are worth more according to the Law of Diminishing Marginal Utility.

Problem Solving Examples:

 What is meant by consumers' surplus?

 The notion of consumers' surplus is the result of two phenomena. First is the idea that people will buy more and more of a particular good or service only at lower and lower cost to them. This is due to the Law of Diminishing Marginal Utility. The second phenomenon is that if a single price prevails in a market, the price consumers pay for each unit of a good or service represents the value they place on the last unit (the marginal unit) bought. Therefore, except for the very last unit purchased, consumers gain more utility from each unit bought than they sacrifice when they purchase it. Since consumers pay only according to the marginal value of the last unit bought, they receive "surplus" of value, from all prior units, which have higher (marginal) utilities than the last unit bought.

Q The diagram shows a market equilibrium for a commodity. Show graphically the total consumer surplus derived by the buyers of this commodity.

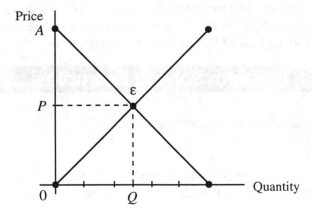

A In any transaction, the consumer's surplus is the measure of the benefit to the consumer over and above his cost. Graphically the total benefit to the consumer of quantity $0Q$ of the commodity can be measured by the area of $0A\varepsilon Q$. The amount paid by the consumer is $0P\varepsilon Q$. The portion of the total benefit over and above the cost is the area $0A\varepsilon Q - 0P\varepsilon Q = PA\varepsilon$. Therefore, consumer surplus can be shown graphically as the area $PA\varepsilon$ as shown.

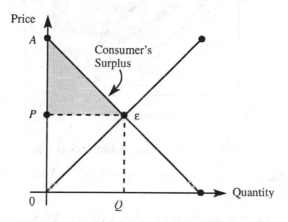

2.15 Appendix: Trade, Edgeworth Box, Contract Curves

Note: *IC*'s of an individual illustrate *trade potential/benefits.* Individual will not trade in shaded region.

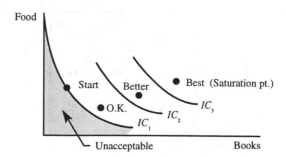

Figure 2.27

Edgeworth Box

Edgeworth Box represents trade between two persons (A, B) for two goods (food, books).

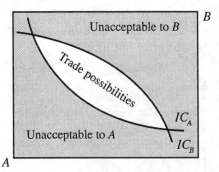

Figure 2.28

- Superimposed A's and B's "trade potential" graphs.

- **Box Shape:** Because the total supplies of food/books is fixed, individuals must go to A or B.

- Trade must be mutually beneficial. Utility of both people must be at a higher level, thus higher IC's must be reached, helping both A and B, or one without hurting the other.

Contract Curve

Contract Curve—Tangency points (IC_A, IC_B) of Edgeworth Box.

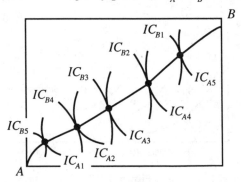

Figure 2.29

All points on the contract curve are Pareto efficient, so that A and B can no longer trade at other points, to make one better off without the other being worse off.

Quiz: Consumer Theory

1. Consumer sovereignty means that

   (A) consumers are protected from fraud by the government.

   (B) the government is the primary consumer of goods and services in the economy.

   (C) the state directs the production of consumer goods.

   (D) consumers ultimately determine what goods are produced.

2. If a consumer is to maximize utility, it is necessary and sufficient

   (A) that the bundle of goods he purchases is somewhere on the budget constraint.

   (B) that he purchases as many goods as possible.

   (C) that no inferior goods are purchased.

   (D) that marginal utilities of all the consumed goods per $1 of income are equal to each other.

3. Any two points on a given indifference curve represent

   (A) two ways of consuming the same amount of each good contained in the consumption basket.

   (B) combinations of goods a consumer can purchase which give him the same total amount of utility.

   (C) the optimal points of consumption.

    (D) the consumer's lack of preference among the goods he purchases.

4.   Suppose two goods are substitutes. Other things being equal, when the price of one of them rises

    (A) the demand for a second good will rise.

    (B) the demand for a second good will fall.

    (C) the price of a second good will also rise.

    (D) the price of a second good will fall.

5.   A budget line of a given consumer shifted outward. This means

    (A) the indifference curve tangent to a new budget line lies everywhere above the previous indifference curve.

    (B) the consumer's real income has increased.

    (C) a consumer is better off.

    (D) All of the above.

6.   The substitution effect alone would imply that the indifference curves

    (A) have a convex shape.

    (B) are straight lines.

    (C) have a concave shape.

    (D) have an irregular shape.

7.   Consider a world where only two goods are available for consumption. Neither one of the goods is assumed to be inferior. The price of one of them falls and consequently a second good becomes relatively more expensive.

    (A) A consumer will necessarily reduce his purchases of a second good.

(B) A consumer will purchase more or less of a second good depending on the relative strengths of the income and substitution effects.

(C) A consumer will be likely to increase his purchases of a second good.

(D) The consumer will not change the amount purchased of both goods.

8. With increases in income, demand for superior/normal goods

(A) decreases.

(B) increases.

(C) remains constant.

(D) None of the above.

9. A Giffen Good is a very strong

(A) superior good.

(B) normal good.

(C) inferior good.

(D) None of the above.

10. The difference between the total utility derived from the consumption of a certain amount of a given good and the amount of money actually paid for it is called

(A) marginal utility.

(B) average utility.

(C) consumer surplus.

(D) producer surplus.

ANSWER KEY

1. (D)
2. (D)
3. (B)
4. (A)
5. (D)

6. (A)
7. (B)
8. (B)
9. (C)
10. (C)

CHAPTER 3

Production—Revenue and Cost

3.1 Production and Efficiency

Production is a process through which resources and/or other products are transformed into different products either for final use or use in another production process. Production also includes services, such as transportation.

Production Function—given the current state of technology, the production function is a physical relationship between a firm's inputs and its output.

Example: $Q = f(L, K, \text{labor, time}, \ldots)$.

Production Possibility is the maximum output from given inputs with a given level of technology.

Technological Efficiency—given the current state of technology, technological efficiency is the production process that requires the least amount of inputs in order to produce a particular level of output.

Economic Efficiency—the goal here is the least-cost production. For a specific rate of output, economic efficiency is the production process that utilizes the lowest per unit cost, for that rate of output. In a competitive market, firms that continue to exist must be economically efficient. Economic efficiency is closely tied to technical efficiency.

Efficient production does not assume that perfect knowledge exists, but that whatever knowledge does exist is being used.

Productivity—the amount of output that is produced by one unit of input. It is measured by units of output per unit of input.

3.1.1 Determinants of Productivity Growth

1. **Economies of Scale**—cases in which the percentage increase in output is greater than the percentage increase of inputs used to produce that output.

2. **Factor Substitution**—substitution of a less productive input for a more productive input.

3. **Improved Quality of Inputs**—e.g., education of labor.

4. **Technological Change**—technological change in one industry generally results in improved ability to obtain more of all goods.

Problem Solving Example:

 What are the major determinants of productivity increases? Briefly describe each.

 The more important determinants or causes of productivity increases can be grouped into four categories as follows:

(1) increasing returns to scale

(2) factor substitution

(3) increasing quality of factors

(4) technological progress

We have increasing returns to scale if output rises by more than 50 percent when all inputs are increased by 50 percent. The significant point here is that in those industries in which economies of scale or returns to scale exist (where an increase in all the factor inputs causes a more than proportionate increase in output), productivity increases as the economy grows. Here population increase or higher disposable per capita income will increase demand, and this will enable firms to take advantage of the economies of scale possible within their existing technology. Also, increased demand for firms' products may allow them to increase productivity by adopting different and more sophisticated organizing techniques — possibly involving mass production.

A second determinant of productivity growth is the substitution of a more productive factor for one that is less productive. This may involve substitution within a factor category (one machine for another, or one type of skilled worker for another) or between different factors, such as capital for land or for labor. Significant productivity gains have occurred from the substitution of capital for labor, and when labor is provided with more efficient capital, fewer workers are required to produce the same amount of output. The resulting decrease in cost will normally yield a decrease in price and thus, in turn, an increase in the quantity demanded — possibly to the degree that more workers will be hired. Of course, the substitution of capital for labor may not always lead to a price decrease. The new capital equipment may cost more, the remaining workers may be successful in bargaining for higher wages, and firms' owners may take higher profits. In that case, the industry would experience a constant level of output, less employment of labor, and higher returns to individual factor units.

A third determinant of productivity increases is improvement in the quality of factors. Companies may discover higher grades of raw materials or better land for special purposes; more sophisticated capital equipment may be developed; and labor's quality may be greatly enhanced through training and education.

Finally, technological progress — the advance in knowledge of the industrial arts that permits new methods of production and new products — is a major determinant of productivity gains. Technological change creates demand for new or improved products and thereby gives rise to economics of scale. The substitution of capital for labor may likely be a result of a technological advance in a capital good. And the quality improvement in either land, capital, or labor may be a function of technological progress.

3.1.2 Factors of Production

Four Major Factors of Production (economic resources) (See Section 1.2.1) land (L), labor (N), capital (K), entrepreneurial ability.

Labor—considered to be the single most important input in U.S., as wages account for more than 80% of labor investment.

High labor productivity is due to:

1. Capital.

2. Natural Resources.

3. Technology.

4. Labor Quality (health, morale, training, education, and aptness).

5. Intangibles (management, market size, environment).

Human Capital—investment in education, training, health, etc.

Division of Labor—creates efficiency and productivity. A task is broken into specialized tasks, allowing each worker to become more skilled in a particular job.

Benefits: greater output with less hours worked.

Cost: work perceived as dull, insignificant part of a whole.

Capital Widening—the duplication of capital goods to meet the increased labor force (capital per worker remains constant).

Capital Deepening—each worker is given more capital inputs in order to raise productivity (capital per worker increases).

Problem Solving Example:

 What is meant by "economic resources" or "factors of production"? Name three categories of resources.

Economic resources, also called factors of production, include all natural, artificial and human resources which may be used in the production or provision of goods or services. For example, economic resources would include crude oil lying under the surface of the earth, the drilling and pumping equipment used to bring it to the surface, the pipeline which carries it to the dock, the ship (and its crew) which transports it to the refinery, the refinery and its workers and supervisors, the tank farm in which refined gasoline is stored, the truck (and its driver) which transports it to the service station, the service station at which it is sold to consumers (including the land on which it is situated, the building and pumps), and the attendant who pumps it into customers' cars.

Three basic categories into which economic resources, or factors of production, may be classified are land, labor and capital. Some economists (for example, McConnell) consider entrepreneurial ability, or "enterprise", to be a fourth category of economic resource.

3.2 Isoquants, Isocost, and Ridge Lines

3.2.1 Returns to Scale and the Production Function–Homogeneity

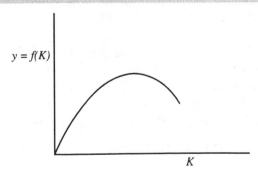

$y = f(K)$

K

Figure 3.1 Production Function

A graph of a production function with one input is given on the previous page. The production function shows **diminishing returns to scale** because output is increasing at a decreasing rate and eventually falls as the input increases.

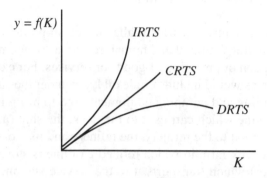

Figure 3.2 Returns to Scale

Returns to Scale are defined in Section 1.6.2. Returns to Scale can be determined by looking at the degree of homogeneity of the production function. Given a production function, $Q = f(K, N)$, it is homogeneous of degree n if $f(xk, XN) = X^n f(K, N)$, where X is a positive number and n is constant. The production function shows constant returns to scale if $n = 1$, increasing returns to scale if $n > 1$, and decreasing returns to scale if $0 < n < 1$.

Problem Solving Example:

Distinguish between the diminishing returns to a factor input and diminishing returns to scale.

The fact that a certain production process is characterized by diminishing returns to a given factor input means that beyond some level of output each successive unit of a given factor added, while the amounts of all other factor inputs are being held constant, will result in smaller and smaller additions to the total output produced.

Diminishing returns to scale describe the tendency of extra output (again, beyond a certain output level) produced as a result of each successive increase of all factor inputs by a certain number, say 2 (all inputs doubled), to become smaller and smaller. The essential difference is that in the case of returns to a factor all the inputs but one are assumed to be fixed while when the returns to scale are considered, all the inputs without exception are allowed to change simultaneously.

3.2.2 The Production or Output Isoquant

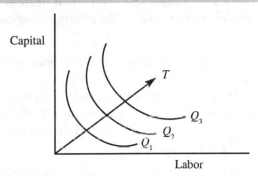

Figure 3.3 Isoquants

Output Isoquants are curves showing all the combinations of inputs that will give the same output.

The curves Q_1, Q_2, and Q_3 are isoquants. Each isoquant corresponds to a given output level. Movements along an isoquant show different input combinations for a given level of output. The ray T from the origin shows increasing output as you move farther from the origin. These isoquants reflect a single production process. Different production processes may require different combinations of inputs to produce a given level of output.

3.2.3 Substitution Among Inputs

The slope of the isoquant is given by the **Marginal Rate of Technical Substitution (MRTS)**.

The marginal rate of technical substitution of b for a ($MRTS_{ba}$) is the amount of b that can be given up for one unit of a in order to keep output constant.

$$MRTS_{ba} = \frac{1}{n}\frac{\Delta b}{\Delta a} = \frac{MP_a}{MP_b}$$

where $MP_a(MP_b)$ is the marginal product of a (b). The **Marginal Product** is the change in input for a unit change of the input.

The isoquant is shaped in such a way that eventually a great deal of one input is needed to compensate for a small decrease in the other input. This is due to the principal of diminishing marginal rate of substitution.

Isoquants reflect complementarity and substitutability between the input factors. The curvature of the isoquant may give us a measure of substitutability. If the isoquants were straight negatively sloped lines, then the two inputs would be perfect substitutes. If the isoquants were right angled, that is they have to be used in fixed quantities, then the two inputs would not be substitutes.

This measure of substitutability can be expressed by the **elasticity of technical substitution** and is measured by the following formula:

$$\sigma = \frac{\text{relative change in the ratio between inputs}}{\text{relative change in the } MRTS_{KL}}$$

$$\sigma = \frac{\Delta(L/K)/(L/K)}{\Delta MRTS_{KL}/MRTS_{KL}}$$

Note: If s = 0, inputs used in fixed proportions.
If s = ∞, factors are perfect substitutes.

3.2.4 Ridge Lines

Ridge Lines are locus points on isoquants where those isoquants turn back on themselves.

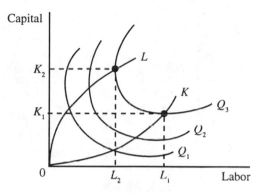

Figure 3.4

Ridge line OK shows the minimum amount of capital for different quantities of output. Ridge line OL shows the minimum amount of labor for different quantities of output. If you have K_1 amount of capital, then no matter how much more labor over L_1 you have, you cannot produce more than Q_3 amount of output; in fact, output will actually decline due to the Law of Diminishing Returns. Therefore, any more labor than L_1, given capital endowment of K_1, will have $MP_L < 0$. Any amount of labor less than L_1, given capital endowment of K_1, will have $MP_L > 0$. Therefore, ridge line OK shows all points where $MP_L = 0$ and ridge line OL shows all points where $MP_K = 0$. The area between the ridge lines is the economical area of production.

3.2.5   The Isocost Curve

The **Isocost Curve** shows different combinations of two given inputs that can be purchased for a certain amount of money, given the nominal prices of these two inputs.

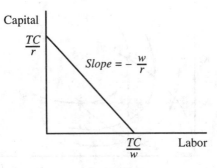

Figure 3.5

w = wage rate

r = interest rate, price of capital

$\dfrac{TC}{r}$ = maximum amount of capital that can be purchased.

$\dfrac{TC}{w}$ = maximum amount of labor that can be purchased.

3.2.6   The Least Cost Combination

The firm wants to reach its highest isoquant given its isocost. This is where the isocost is tangent to an isoquant, where:

$$MRTS_{K,L} = \frac{MP_L}{MP_K} = \frac{P_L}{P_K} = \frac{w}{r}$$

$\Rightarrow$ the least cost combination.

Graphically it looks like:

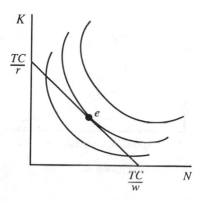

Figure 3.6

Point e is where $\dfrac{MP_L}{MP_K} = \dfrac{w}{r}$.

3.3 Product Curves

Total Physical Product (TP)—the total physical output that is pro
duced in any given production process.

Average Physical Product (AP)—TP/inputs used.

Marginal Physical Product (MP)—definition given in Section 3.2.3.

Law of Diminishing Marginal Physical Product

Holding fixed inputs constant and just increasing the one variable
input beyond a certain point will result in a decreasing marginal product. For instance, increasing the labor force while holding capital at a
constant level will produce higher output, but the additional output per
man-hour will become smaller and smaller as more labor is added.

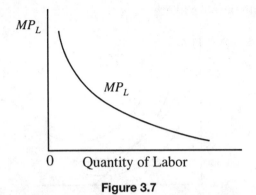

0   Quantity of Labor

Figure 3.7

3.3.1 The Geometry of the TP, MP, and AP Relationships

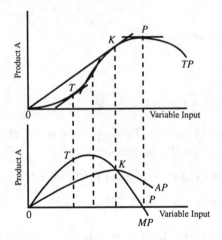

Figure 3.8 The TP, MP, and AP Curves

- The *AP* is the measurement of the slope connecting a given point on the *TP* curve with the origin.

- The *MP* is the measurement of the slope of *TP* at any point on that curve.

Problem Solving Example:

Q Using the data provided in the accompanying table, compute the marginal and average physical productivities. What is the "optimum" population (level of population with highest per capita income) for this economy?

Population (Thousands)	Total Physical Product (Thousand Tons)	Marginal Physical Product (Thousand Tons)	Average Physical Product (Tons)
1	10	–	–
2	22	–	–
3	36	–	
4	52	–	–
5	70	–	–
6	90	–	–
7	108	–	
8	124	–	–
9	135	–	

A The marginal physical product per thousand people is computed by determining how much the total physical product is increased by the addition of an extra thousand people to the economy. So, when the first 1,000 people arrive, they have a marginal physical product of 10,000 tons. When the second 1,000 people arrive, 12,000 tons (22 – 10) are added to the total physical product. The marginal physical productivity of this group, then, is 12,000 tons. This process is repeated to compute the other marginal productivities.

The average physical product is computed by dividing the total physical production by the corresponding total population. So, for the first 1,000 people, the average physical product is ten tons. For 2,000 people, the average physical product is 11 tons per thousand. By repeating this process for the other levels of population, the following table is obtained:

Population (Thousands)	Total Physical Product (Thousand Tons)	Marginal Physical Product (Thousand Tons)	Average Physical Product (Tons)
1	12	10	10 $(\frac{10}{1})$
2	22	12 $(22-10)$	11 $(\frac{22}{2})$
3	36	14 $(36-22)$	12 $(\frac{36}{3})$
4	52	16 $(52-36)$	13 $(\frac{52}{4})$
5	70	18 $(70-52)$	14 $(\frac{70}{5})$
6	90	20 $(90-70)$	15 $(\frac{90}{6})$
7	108	18 $(108-90)$	15.4 $(\frac{108}{7})$
8	124	16 $(124-108)$	15.5 $(\frac{124}{8})$
9	135	11 $(135-124)$	15 $(\frac{135}{9})$

To determine the optimum population, find the level of population that has the highest average physical product. The average physical product is simply another way of saying per capita output, or per capita income. So per capita income (average physical product) is highest when the population is 8,000 people, with a per capita income of 15.5 tons of product. Note that the average physical product is not highest where marginal physical product is highest. Average physical product continues to rise after marginal physical product has started to fall, because marginal product (18 with 7,000 people) is still higher than average product (15.4 with 7,000 people). Average product will rise whenever it is less than marginal product, even if marginal product is decreasing.

3.3.2   The Three Stages of Production

1st Stage—The first stage of production is from the point 0 to *T* in Figure 3.3.2. At point *T*, *MP* changes from increasing to decreasing.

2nd Stage—The second stage of production is from point *T* to point *K*. Point *K* is where *MP* = *AP*.

3rd Stage—The third stage is from point *K* to point *P*. Point *P* is where *TP* is at its maximum point, that is, where *MP* = 0.

Stages 1 and 3 are called uneconomic regions of production. Stage 2 is the economic region of production.

3.4   Revenue

Total Revenue (TR)—Maximum receipts obtainable by selling a given quantity of output per unit of time.

$$TR = P X Q$$

measured in dollars

Average Revenue (AR)

$$AR = \frac{TR}{Q}$$

measured in dollars

Marginal Revenue (MR)—Change in *TR* caused by one unit change in output sold.

$$MR = \frac{\Delta TR}{\Delta Q}$$

Marginal Revenue Product (MRP)–A change in total revenue that results from a one unit change in some variable input with other inputs held constant.

$$MRP = MR \times MP$$

Problem Solving Example:

In a price-takers' market, does the marginal revenue of each seller equal the average revenue (price)? Why?

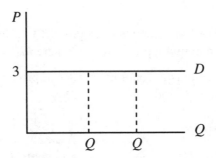

Yes, under the conditions of perfect competition, which imply that all the producers are price-takers, the marginal revenue of each seller equals the average revenue or the price of a product.

A producer can sell any amount of output at the market price (see figure). This is precisely the meaning of the horizontal demand schedule a producer is facing (see figure). Marginal revenue is simply the revenue obtained from the sale of the last unit of output. In case of a price-taker, no matter what quantity he chooses to produce, the last unit will still be sold at the prevailing market price of $3 (see figure). Therefore, marginal revenue of our producer will always be $5 which is the price of a product and also, of course, average revenue received from the sale of any amount of output.

3.5 Cost

3.5.1 Definitions

Economic Cost—Value of the alternative that is being given up in order to obtain some specific item. Economic Cost is the same as **Opportunity Cost** (See Section 1.3).

Explicit Cost—Monetary payments going out of the firm.

Implicit Cost (non-expenditures)—Cost associated with the usage of the resources that the firm owns.

Depreciation—Decrease in the value of a capital good due to wear or obsolescence.

Private Cost—All implicit and explicit cost encountered by a person or a firm.

Social Cost—Private cost plus any other extraneous cost (externality) accrued by the members of the society which are infringed on by some trading parties. An example of an externality is pollution.

Short Run (SR)—Time period too short to change all inputs (i.e., plant size), but long enough to change some inputs (i.e., labor).

Long Run (LR)—*All* inputs are variable.

Fixed Cost (FC)—"Sunk Cost," cost not varying with the rate of output. Fixed costs occur even when output is zero (e.g., contracts, rent, etc.). Disregard FC when deciding what quantity to produce in the short run since FC's between two production levels cancel out.

Variable Cost (VC)—Costs that vary with the quantity produced (e.g., wages, materials, etc.).

Total Cost (TC)—All costs associated with producing a given quantity.

$$TC = TFC + TVC$$

where TFC = Total Fixed Cost

TVC = Total Variable Cost

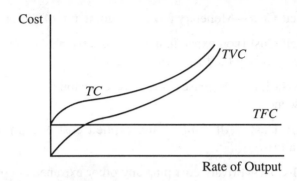

Figure 3.9 Total Cost, Total Fixed Cost, Total Variable Cost

Marginal Cost (MC)—The change in the TC due to a one-unit change in the rate of output.

$$MC = \frac{\Delta TC}{\Delta Q}$$

There is a direct relation between the marginal product of an input and the marginal cost. For example, let

r = rental price of capital

K = quantity of capital used per unit of time

As we increase the amount of capital, total cost increases as well as total output.

$$MC = \frac{\Delta TC}{\Delta Q} = \frac{r\Delta K}{\Delta Q} = r\left(\frac{1}{\Delta Q / \Delta K}\right)$$

$\dfrac{\Delta Q}{\Delta K}$ is the marginal product of capital, MP_K. Therefore,

$MC = r\left(\dfrac{1}{MP_K}\right)$. Due to the law of diminishing marginal productivity, we have increasing marginal cost in the short run. This is why the marginal cost curve must eventually rise in the short run. However, at first the marginal cost curve can decline due to increasing returns to scale.

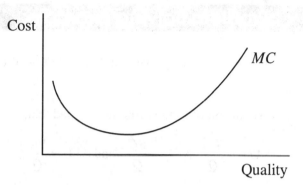

Figure 3.10 The Marginal Cost Curve

– Increasing Returns ($\uparrow MP$) are reflected in decreasing marginal cost.

– Decreasing Returns ($\downarrow MP$) are reflected in increasing marginal cost.

Average Total Cost

$$ATC = \frac{TC}{Q} = AFC + AVC$$

where AFC = Average Fixed Cost

AVC = Average Variable Cost

$TVC = KP_K$

$$AVC = \frac{KP_K}{Q} = \frac{P_K}{Q/K} = \frac{P_K}{AP_K}$$

Problem Solving Example:

Given $TC = FC + VC$, prove that $ATC = AFC + AVC$.

To solve this proof it must first be recalled that:

$$ATC = \frac{TC}{Q}, \ AFC = \frac{FC}{Q}, \text{ and } AVC = \frac{VC}{Q}.$$

With this in mind, the given equation is multiplied by 1/Q to get:

$$\frac{TC}{Q} = \frac{FC}{Q} + \frac{VC}{Q}$$

which, by the definitions, is equivalent to ATC = AFC + AVC.

Intuitively, this equation means that cost per unit may be divided up into two parts, AFC, or the portion of fixed cost attributed to any one unit of output, and AVC, or the portion of variable cost attributed to any one unit of output.

3.5.2 The Long Run Cost Curves

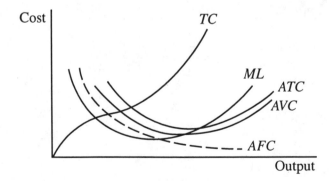

Figure 3.11

- The Total Cost Curve is *S*-shaped and continually rises.

- The *AFC* continually falls as output rises.

- The *AVC* falls and eventually rises because of the changes in marginal cost.

- The distance between the *ATC* and *AVC* decreases as output grows.

The geometric relationship between *TC, ATC,* and *MC* is essentially the same as the geometric relationship between *TP, AP,* and *MP* (see section 3.3.1).

3.5.3 The Short Run Cost Curves

In the long run all inputs are variable, but in the short run some inputs are fixed. An example of a fixed input is plant size. For each different plant size, we have a different short run average cost curve that goes with it.

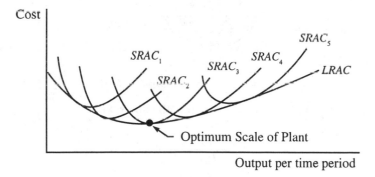

Figure 3.12

Each *SRAC* curve in Figure 3.12 corresponds to a different plant size. The Long Run Average Cost Curve (*LRAC*) "envelops" the *SRAC* curves.

The point where one of the *SRAC* curves is tangent to the *LRAC* curve at its lowest point is the optimum scale of the plant. This is the point where the *LRAC* curve is also at its lowest. The *LRAC* curve shows the least cost of producing a given level of output, thus, it reflects every point where

$$\frac{MP_K}{P_K} = \frac{MP_L}{P_L}$$

Another way to look at the difference between the *SRAC* and *LRAC* would be to look at the **Expansion Path.** The expansion path shows how the inputs increase as the desired level of output increases, keeping the ratio of input factor prices constant.

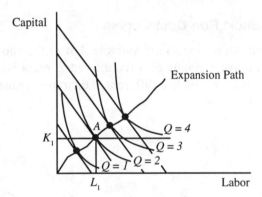

Figure 3.13 The Expansion Path

Each point along the expansion path shows where

$$\frac{MP_K}{P_K} = \frac{MP_L}{P_L}.$$

Now suppose *K* was fixed at K_1. To produce output level 1, it would cost more in the short run than in the long run, less labor would be needed. But to produce output level 2, the total outlay would be the same in the long run as it is in the short run. At point *A*, the same amount of capital and labor is used in the short run and long run. Thus, we have a point where the *SRAC* curve is tangent to the *LRAC* curve. At point *A* we have a point on the *LRAC* curve, however, this is not necessarily the low point on the *SRAC* curve as can be seen in Figure 3.14.

The Short Run Marginal Cost Curve (*SRMC*) also differs from the Long Run Marginal Cost Curve (*LRMC*) for the same reasons that *SRAC* differs from *LRAC*.

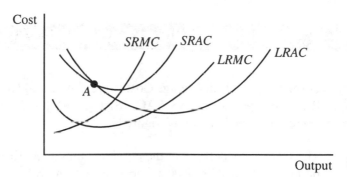

Figure 3.14

Problem Solving Examples:

 Could a Short Run Average Cost Curve ever contain a point below the Long Run Average Cost Curve? Why or why not?

The Long Run Average Cost curve (LRAC) traces out the lowest possible average cost for any given quantity produced, under the assumption that every input into the production process is variable, including, among other things, plant size and machinery. Any given Short Run Average Cost Curve (SRAC) shows the lowest possible average cost for each quantity produced, assuming that at least one input is held constant. The example most commonly used to illustrate this point is plant size. For example, if a producer is currently producing in a factory designed to produce 100,000 units most efficiently, then this factory will produce 80,000 units less efficiently, that is, at a higher cost per unit, than would a factory designed to produce exactly 80,000 units.

Using these definitions, it is impossible for a SRAC to ever contain a point below its LRAC. If some point on a SRAC could produce at lower per-unit costs then this point would be included in the LRAC. Therefore, since only the lowest possible average costs for any given quantity produced are included on the LRAC, the SRAC will never contain a point below the LRAC.

Problem Solving Example:

Q Given the Long Run Average Cost curve, LAC, could the Short Run Average Cost curves SAC_1, SAC_2, SAC_3 and SAC_4 all correspond to the given LAC in the figure?

A The LAC is, by definition, the curve containing all the lowest points on the SAC's. That is, no point on any SAC may fall below the LAC. Therefore, SAC_1 and SAC_4 cannot be Short Run Average Cost curves associated with the LAC in the figure.

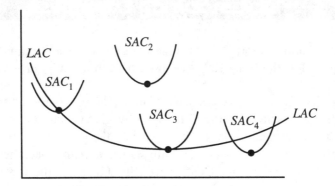

SAC_2 does not touch LAC at any point. This means that for any given quantity produced there exists some SAC, some combination of inputs, which will produce the product at a lower cost per unit (AC) than any point on SAC_2. While it is possible that a manufacturer would construct a factory that is less efficient at all levels of output than some other factory might be, this is generally not assumed to be the case. Therefore, SAC_2 would not really be a Short Run Average Cost curve associated with LAC. SAC_3 touches LAC at one point, and it does not contain any points which lie below LAC. That is, it represents an efficient combination of inputs but not more efficient than is possible in the Long Run. Therefore, SAC_3 is the only one of the four Short Run curves drawn that corresponds to LAC.

3.5.4 The Multiple Plant Firm

The firm wishes to distribute its output among its several plants as it tries to minimize the cost of producing a given level of output. It will allocate its output according to each plant's marginal cost of producing the output. The firm will distribute its output in such a way that the MC of all its plants will be equal. This can be seen in the following figure:

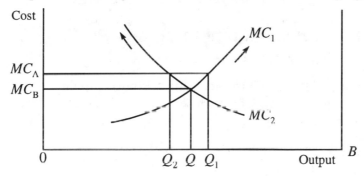

Figure 3.15 A Two Plant Firm

where MC_1 increases from left to right and MC_2 increases from right to left. The total cost for the firm could be minimized if plant 1 (with Marginal Cost Curve MC_1) produces $0Q$ and plant 2 (with Marginal Cost Curve MC_2) produces BQ.

Suppose plant 1 produces $0Q_1$ and plant 2 produces the remainder, BQ_1. It can be shown that this is *not* the minimum cost for the output $0B$. If you decrease output for plant 1 by one unit ($Q_1 - Q$), then cost will fall by MC_A. If you increase output for plant 2 by one unit so that total output remains unchanged, cost will go up by MC_B. Therefore, by transferring a unit of output from plant 1 to plant 2, total cost will fall by $MC_A - MC_B$. The reverse can be seen if plant 2 produces BQ_2 and plant 2 produces $0Q_2$.

CHAPTER 4

Perfect Competition

4.1 Perfect Competition and Profit Maximization

Normal Profit (Π) (or Accounting Profit)—Minimum profit required in the long run for a producer to be willing to stay in business; treated as an implicit cost.

$$\Pi = TR - TC$$

where TR = Total Revenue and

TC = Total Cost

Profit Maximization—Fundamental goal of the producers as utility maximization is for the consumers.

Perfect Competition (PC)—Market structure characterized by the following properties:

1. Large number of independent buyers and sellers.

2. Homogeneity of products (products are non-differentiable).

3. Firms are price-takers — individual firms cannot influence price.

4. Free entry and exit of firms into (and out of) the industry.

5. Perfect information.

6. No constraint on the movement of prices.

Perfect competition is *rare* in practice but is important for study because it represents a useful, relative approximation of how markets operate. It also makes it easier to predict how certain economic policies will work in the real world.

Problem Solving Examples:

 Define perfect competition.

Perfect competition occurs in a market with numerous buyers and sellers exchanging a homogeneous product, and with free entry into the market for this product. Because there are so many buyers and sellers, no one person or firm has any influence over the price; they are all "price-takers." There is only a single homogeneous product in the market, and consumers of the product possess complete information regarding the price charged by all the producing firms, so no firm can charge a higher price than any other firm without losing all its customers. So the demand conditions for each firm are the same. No firm has an advantage from brand-name recognition.

Free entry in (and exit from) the market make it impossible for firms to earn economic profits in the long run. If there are economic profits being made, additional firms will enter the industry. They will continue to enter until there are so many firms that no one firm can earn any more than "normal" profits on its operations. Any industry that has these three characteristics (numerous buyers and sellers, a homogeneous product, and free entry) is called perfectly competitive.

What are the conditions necessary for perfect competition?

The conditions are

a) that there are many buyers and sellers in the market;

b) that no single buyer or seller is able to influence the price of the good;

c) that the product is standardized and uniform;

d) that new firms are free to enter and existing firms are free to leave the industry; and

e) that there is virtually no room for nonprice competition.

4.2 The Demand Curve for a Perfectly Competitive Firm

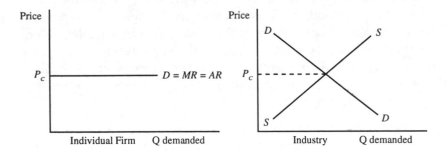

Figure 4.1

− A firm is a price-taker in the Perfectly Competitive market.

− If a firm faces a horizontal demand, it can sell any quantity it wants at price P_c; but if it charges more than P_c, it will sell zero output.

The **Marginal Revenue (MR)** for any firm is given by

$$MR = AR - \frac{AR}{\eta} = P\left(1 - \frac{1}{\eta}\right)$$

where η is the price elasticity of demand (see Section 1.9.1). Since the demand curve that each individual firm faces in a perfectly competitive market is horizontal, $\eta = -\infty$. Therefore, $MR = P(1 + 1/-\infty) = P(1 + 0) = P$. The *MR* for a competitive firm is equal to the price of the good. So the marginal revenue curve for a perfect competitor is a horizontal line.

Problem Solving Examples:

 What is marginal revenue? How does the elasticity of demand affect marginal revenue?

Marginal revenue is defined as the change in total revenue that results from an increase in quantity demanded by one unit. Suppose we have the following excerpt from a company's demand schedule:

	Quantity demanded	Price
A.	8	$11
B.	9	$10

In case A, Total Revenue = Price × Quantity demanded = $11 × 8 = $88. In case B, Total Revenue = $10 × 9 = $90. Then since marginal revenue is the change in total revenue as quantity demanded increases by one unit, marginal revenue = $90 − $88 = $2.

One way to study elasticity of demand is in relation to total revenue. We saw when first considering demand elasticity, that if demand is elastic, total revenue increases as price falls. Now a falling price is equivalent to a rising quantity demanded (due to the downward-sloping nature of demand curves). Therefore, if demand is elastic, total revenue will increase as quantity demanded increases and marginal revenue will be positive if demand is elastic.

Similarly, if demand is inelastic, total revenue decreases as price falls. Therefore, total revenue decreases as quantity demanded is increased and marginal revenue is negative.

Finally, if demand is unitarily elastic, total revenue does not change as price is maneuvered. Therefore, marginal revenue is zero.

 Which of the curves represents the demand faced by a producer under perfect competition?

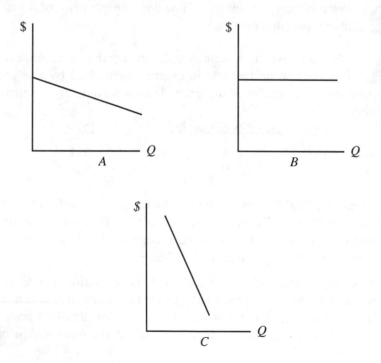

A A perfectly competitive firm is one that is so small compared to the size of the entire market that it cannot affect market price regardless of how much it decides to supply. That is, whether the perfect competitor supplies nothing (Q = 0) or the maximum that he can produce, market price will always be the same to him. Note that the demand curves *A* and *C* both show that as the producer increases his output, i.e., moves to the right along the Q-axis, the price offered to him declines. Therefore *A* and *C* do not represent demand to a perfectly competitive firm. Demand curve *B* shows a constant price, regardless of the quantity of output level chosen. Therefore, *B*, a horizontal line, does show demand to a perfectly competitive firm.

4.3 Profit Maximization Under Perfect Competition—Short Run

4.3.1 Total Revenue/Total Cost Analysis

$$\text{Profit} = \Pi = TR - TC$$

max Π = max positive difference between *TR* and *TC*. If the *TR* curve is a straight ray from the origin, a firm is necessarily a price-taker.

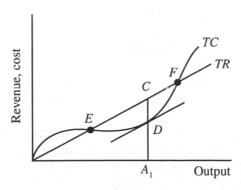

Figure 4.2

Breakeven Points—Points where no profits or losses are made. This is where $TR = TC$, at points E and F.

Profit Maximization—Π-Max rate of output occurs at A_1 where the gap between TR and TC is the greatest. This occurs where the slope of the TC curve (MC) is equal to the slope of the TR curve (MR) and TR is greater than TC.

Problem Solving Example:

 Given, in the figure below, the total cost and total revenue curves for a perfectly competitive firm,

a) Explain why total revenue is a straight line.

b) Show the range where profits can be realized.

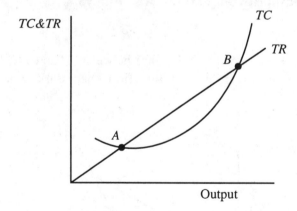

Output

a) We know from theory that under perfect competition, the demand curve faced by a firm is horizontal, i.e., the price that the market will pay is constant. Total revenue (TR) is defined as price × quantity, and since price is constant, $TR = cQ$, where $c = P$. We can see that this equation is a straight line with slope $= c$.

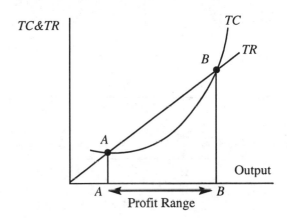

b) Profits will be realized as long as $TR \geq TC$. When $TR = TC$, we say that the firm is realizing a normal profit. We also call this the break-even point. Looking at the graph we see that $TC = TR$ (the two graphs intersect) at points A and B. In the interval between points A and B, $TR > TC$. Therefore, the firm is realizing excess profits here. At any point to the left of A or to the right of B, $TC > TR$. So at these points, the company would incur a loss.

Therefore, the range of profits is from Output = A to Output = B, as shown in the figure.

4.3.2 Marginal Revenue/Marginal Cost Analysis

Since the slope of the TR is Marginal Revenue (MR) and the slope of the TC curve is Marginal Cost (MC), profit maximization occurs where $MR = MC$. This is true for any market (i.e., monopoly, oligopoly, competition, etc.). But for the competitive market, we know that $MR = P$, so Π_{max} is where $MR = P = MC$.

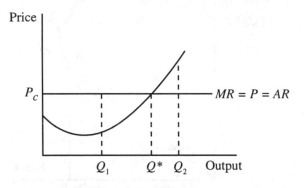

Figure 4.3

–   At output Q_1, the firm is producing where $MR > MC$. The firm can increase profits by producing more units because the increased revenue from that good will exceed the increase in the cost to produce that good. The firm can increase profits by the area in between the MR and MC curves and Q_1 and Q^*.

–   At output Q_2, the firm is producing where $MC > MR$. The firm could increase profits if it *decreases* its output. This is because the decrease in cost will be greater than the decrease in revenue.

–   At output Q^*, the firm is producing where $MC = MR$. The firm cannot increase profit by producing more or less, so this is the profit maximizing output for the firm.

The firm's objective is to maximize the total Π, (as shown by the shaded area in the following graph) and not the average profit (Π/unit) (as read along vertical axis). Average profit would be maximized at minimum average cost.

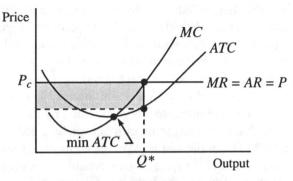

Figure 4.4

Problem Solving Example:

In the figure below, *MC* shows Astro Corporation's (a perfect competitor) Marginal Costs of producing commodity A. P_M represents the market price of A. Why wouldn't Astro produce quantities Q_S or Q_L? How much of A will they choose to produce?

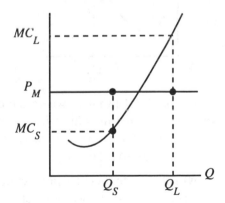

A This question is asking why a producer in a perfectly competitive market should choose not to produce where the cost of the last unit produced (Marginal Cost) is either greater or less than the market price. Intuitively, if commodity A is selling for $3 per unit, and the last unit of output cost only $2.00 to produce (don't forget that the economist's definition of cost includes a "normal" profit for the producer) then Astro could increase its net revenues by increasing its production level. Here, by increasing output even by 1 unit, Astro would add $3 - $2 = $1.00 on the last unit produced to its net revenue (total revenue - total cost). By increasing its production level to the point where the cost of producing the last unit of output (MC) was just equal to the price of the good, P_M, Astro would be maximizing its profits (net revenue).

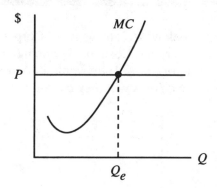

Similarly, Astro would not produce where the cost of producing the last unit of output was greater than the price received for it. That is, if the market price was $3, it wouldn't make sense for Astro to produce an additional unit if it cost $4 to produce.

Since the firm will choose to increase production whenever MC is less than the Price, and it will decrease production whenever MC is greater than the Price, then the point where the firm should produce, as shown by Q_e, will occur where $P = MC$.

4.3.3 The Firm's Short Run Shutdown and Break-Even Points

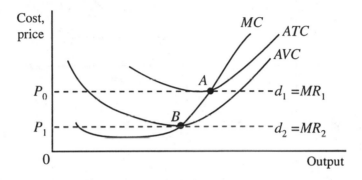

Figure 4.5

- The short run break-even point occurs at point A, where $P_0 = ATC_{min}$; at P_0, total costs are just covered.

- The short run shutdown point occurs at point B, where $P_1 = AVC_{min}$. At any point below this, the firm would not even meet its variable cost and it would minimize any loss by shutting down.

- At any price between P_0 and P_1, the firm will produce in the short run to minimize its loss. But if the price remains below P_0 in the long run, the firm will shut down.

Problem Solving Example:

Q Given the following situations defined by the three different marginal revenue curves, show in what situation a profit would be made, in what situation a loss would occur, and in what case a firm would break even.

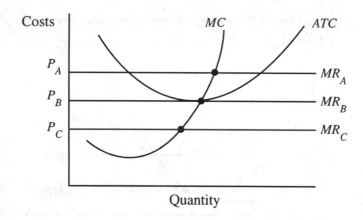

We assume that this firm is profit-maximizing. Therefore, it will produce at the point where $MR = MC$. Under perfect competition, MR = price = average revenue.

If we look at MR_A, we see that at the point at which it intersects MC, Price $P_A > ATC$. That is, since average revenue per unit (P_A) is greater than the average cost per unit, the firm is making a positive profit on every unit sold. Therefore, at this point, profits will be maximized and will be positive.

Looking at MR_B, we see that at the intersection of MC and MR_B, $MC = MR_B$ = Price = ATC. That is, at this point, average revenue per unit (P_B) is the same as average cost per unit and the firm is making neither a profit nor a loss. Therefore, at this point, the firm will break even.

Finally MR_C intersects MC at a quantity where $ATC >$ Price. Therefore, a loss occurs here.

4.3.4 The Supply Curve of the Individual Firm in the Short Run

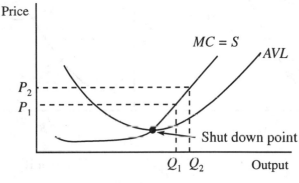

Figure 4.6

The supply curve for this firm is the portion of the MC curve which lies above the AVC curve, i.e., above the shutdown point. Thus, at P_1, Q_1 will be supplied by this firm to consumers. At P_2, Q_2 will be supplied to the consumers.

Problem Solving Example:

Q Graphs I and II represent cost curves for Firms A and B, both perfect competitors, where P_A and P_B represent market price to A and B respectively and Q_A and Q_B represent each firm's output. Are either of these firms making an economic profit or loss? If so, show the amount of this profit or loss in total and on a per-unit basis.

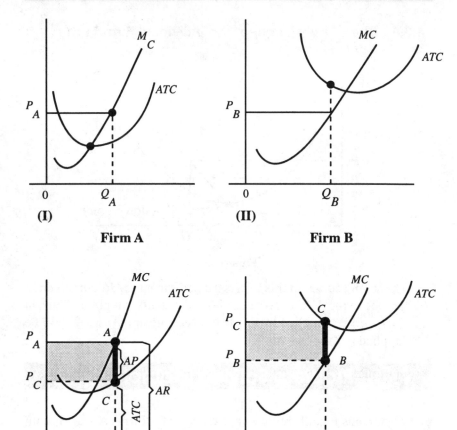

(I) Firm A

(II) Firm B

(III)

(IV)

Economic profits which are also referred to as pure profits or excess profits, are defined as Total Revenue minus Total Cost, $TP = TR - TC$. Where TP is a positive number, ($TR>TC$), the firm is making economic profits. Where TP is negative, ($TR<TC$), the firm is incurring losses. Note, that profit on a per-unit basis, that is, Average Profit (AP), can be determined by dividing TP by Q:

$$AP \equiv \frac{TP}{Q} \equiv \frac{TR}{Q} - \frac{TC}{Q}$$

Remember that $TR/Q \equiv$ Average Revenue (AR) and $TC/Q \equiv$ Average Total Cost (ATC) which gives: $TP/Q = AP = AR - ATC$. When a firm is making profits, AP is a positive number, which implies that AR is greater than ATC. If a firm was incurring losses, then AP would be negative. This would imply that AR was less than ATC.

Keeping this in mind, note in Graph III that for Firm A, at its production level of Q_A, ATC lies below Average Revenue ($AR = TQR = PQ/Q = P$. That is, Firm A is making an economic profit. On a per-unit basis, this profit, Average Profit, can be shown as the difference between the Average Revenue and Average Total Costs at Q_A, or distance AP in Graph III.

Remember that $ATC \times Q = TC$, $AR \times Q = TR$ and $AP \times Q = TP$. Geometrically, one side of a rectangle, multiplied by an adjacent side gives the area of the rectangle. Thus, TC is represented by the rectangle $0P_CCQ_A$, TR is rectangle $0P_AAQ_A$, and TP is rectangle P_CP_AAC. Note that TP could also be determined by subtracting the TC rectangle from the TR rectangle. Thus, geometrically, profit on a per-unit basis to Firm A is the length of line from A to C, while Firm A's Total Profit can be represented by the area of the shaded rectangle P_CP_AAC.

For Firm B, note that the Average Total Cost curve lies above Average Revenue at Q_B. Therefore, $AP = AR - ATC$ is a negative number and Firm B is incurring a loss. Using the same logic as for Firm A, Firm B's loss on a per-unit basis is shown in Graph IV as the distance from C to B, that is, the distance from Q_B to C, ATC, minus the distance from Q_B to B, AR. Firm B's total loss can be shown by the area of the shaded rectangle P_BP_CCB.

4.4 Profit Maximization Under Perfect Competition—Long Run

In the long run, output of the firm can be varied by a change in the scale of the plant. There is ample time for firms to enter and leave the industry. Losses will result in the exit of firms which cannot pay their fixed cost, and economic profit will cause entry of new firms into the industry.

Long run equilibrium occurs where

$$SRMC = LRMC = MR = P = SRAC = LRAC$$

Let's look at the case where the firm is making a profit. Assume the firm is producing where $SRMC = LRMC = MR = P > SRAC = LRAC$. This can be seen in the following graph.

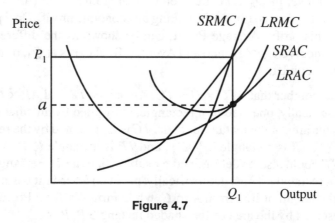

Figure 4.7

The firm is making a profit of $(P_1 - a) \cdot Q_1$. However, other firms see these profits and enter the industry for these profits. This shifts the supply curve for the *industry* to the right and lowers the price. This can be seen in the following graph.

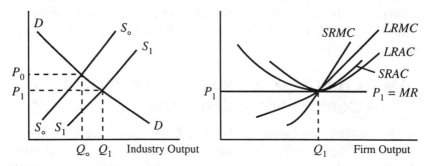

Figure 4.8

A firm will soon find itself in a situation like the right-hand graph of Figure 4.8. In this situation, *no* economic profits or losses will be made.

Note: Zero economic profits ≠ zero accounting profits. What zero economic profits means is that all factors of production are paid their opportunity cost.

If a number of firms in the industry suffer losses in the long run, there will be an exit of such firms from that industry and the industry supply curve will shift back to the left. Prices will rise and output will fall, the opposite of the scenario depicted in the graph.

In this analysis, we placed the entire burden of adjustment on prices. However, as more firms enter the industry, the cost of inputs rises. The following graphs show how the increase in supply affects the firm's cost curves.

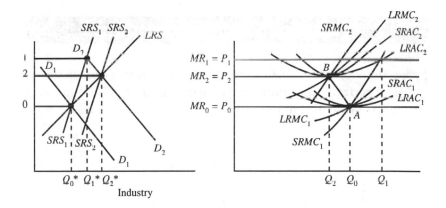

Figure 4.9

The firm and the industry are originally at equilibrium at Q_0. A shift in the demand curve from D_1 to D_2 causes price to rise from P_0 to P_1 where SRS_1 intersects D_2. The firm now attempts to maximize profits where the $SRMC$ intersects the $P_1 = MR_1$ curve. The firm increases its output to Q_1.

But now the firm is making economic profits. This attracts more firms to the industry. Two things will happen:

1. As new firms enter the industry and old firms increase output, the prices of the inputs are bid up, which shifts the cost curves up.

2. As new firms enter the industry, SRS_1 shifts out to SRS_2 and the price declines to P_2.

Now we have a two-way squeeze on profits, one from above as price declines and one from below as costs rise. The new equilibrium for the firm is Q_2 and the new equilibrium for the industry is Q_2^*. Again, at this equilibrium, economic profits are equal to zero. Industry output and prices have increased from the original equilibrium of P_0^* and Q_0^*, but the amount of output from the individual firm has declined from Q_0 to Q_2. Notice that the *long run* supply curve is *BA*, which shows the quantities supplied at various prices after all long run adjustment processes have happened. The long run supply curve for the industry is sloping upward, while the long run supply curve for the firm is sloping downward.

Problem Solving Example:

Q Economists claim that the equilibrium position of each firm in a perfectly competitive industry in industry equilibrium can be pictured as in the diagram.

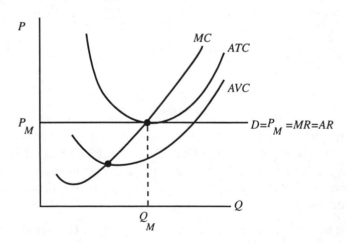

Notice that at the equilibrium market price Average Revenue per unit is exactly equal to Average Cost per unit. This means that $AR \times QM$ is exactly equal to $AC \times Q_M$, which means that Total Revenue is the same as Total Cost. Since Costs and Revenues are exactly the same here, this means that there are no profits. Why would any producer stay in business if there are no profits to be gained from doing so?

A The solution to this problem lies in recalling the economist's definition of Profits. So-called normal profits are included in the cost curves; that is, the owner's salary return on his capital investments and entrepreneurial skills are all included as costs. Therefore, what the layman normally considers a "nice profit," to the economist, is a cost of the firm. The Total Profit obtained by subtracting Total Costs from Total Revenues (TR–TC) is known as "excess profits." Under perfect competition, these excess profits are competed away, but the normal profits remain, keeping the firm in the market.

4.5 Advantages and Disadvantages of Perfect Competition

Advantages:

1. Most efficient production (no waste of resources) and resource utilization (no unemployment).

2. Prices are as low as possible: there is no economic profit—consumers get products at their true cost.

3. Standard Product: there is no need for advertising.

Disadvantages:

1. If producers just cover costs, they cannot worry about such negative externalities as pollution.

2. Firms are too small for large-scale research and development of new technology.

Quiz: Production—Revenue and Cost & Perfect Competition

1. Output isoquants are curves showing all the combinations of inputs that will give the same

    (A) price.

    (B) wage rates.

    (C) output.

    (D) None of the above.

2. Diminishing marginal returns occur

    (A) after some point, as increasing amounts of a factor are added to fixed amounts of other factors of production.

    (B) when the marginal utility of income just equals the marginal utility of leisure, but not before.

    (C) because, basically, as more workers are employed in a plant they talk more and produce less.

    (D) because of the laws of physics and engineering.

    (E) because of the operation of a general economic principle called economies of scale.

3. The marginal revenue product is

    (A) the selling price of the last unit of output.

    (B) the increment of total revenue resulting from the use of an additional unit of input.

    (C) used in determining marginal physical product.

    (D) harder to determine in pure competition than in monopoly.

    (E) harder to determine in pure competition than in oligopoly.

4. Which of the following best describes what explicit costs are?

    (A) Remuneration of self-owned and self-employed resources

    (B) Monetary payments firms make to those who supply labor services, raw materials

    (C) Minimum payments to keep talents in the firm

    (D) Maximum payments to keep talents in the firm

5. A distinguishing characteristic of the long run period is that

    (A) all costs are fixed costs.

    (B) all costs are variable costs.

    (C) fixed costs tend to be greater than variable costs.

    (D) fixed costs tend to be lesser than variable costs.

6. A firm with multiple plants will distribute its output so that the MC of all plants will be

    (A) equal.

    (B) maximized.

    (C) minimized.

    (D) None of the above.

7. Under conditions of pure competition, the firm will maximize profits when

    (A) price and marginal cost are rising.

    (B) average fixed cost is falling.

    (C) price and marginal cost are equated.

    (D) average fixed cost and marginal cost are falling.

    (E) None of the above.

8.   The break-even point for a perfectly competitive firm that is maximizing profits occurs where the price equals

   (A)   the minimum point on the ATC curve.

   (B)   marginal cost.

   (C)   marginal revenue.

   (D)   average revenue.

   (E)   all of the above, simultaneously.

9.   In the long run, as new firms enter an industry and old firms increase output, prices of inputs are bid up which shifts cost curves

   (A)   down.

   (B)   up.

   (C)   horizontally.

   (D)   None of the above.

10.   If prices fall in a perfectly competitive industry, the firms in the industry in the short run will

   (A)   not increase in number.

   (B)   keep output at the same level but make losses.

   (C)   try to reduce production or shut down.

   (D)   advertise.

   (E)   None of the above.

ANSWER KEY

1. (C)	6. (A)
2. (A)	7. (C)
3. (B)	8. (E)
4. (B)	9. (B)
5. (B)	10. (C)

CHAPTER 5

The Monopoly

5.1 Imperfect Competition and Monopoly

In a perfectly competitive market, all resources are optimally allocated; thus, the maximum social benefit is equal to the maximum producer benefit. Although perfect competition is the ideal market structure for society and its consumers, it is not ideal for the producers. Producers would like to be **monopolistic**—the only supplier in the industry. Monopolies arise due to conditions of imperfect competition in the market in which a firm has control over prices. An imperfectly competitive market can also lead to monopolistic competition or an oligopoly.

A *monopoly* has the following properties:

1. There is only one seller.

2. There are no close substitutes.

3. The monopolist is the price setter since the monopolist faces a downward sloping demand curve.

4. There are barriers to entry—the firm, and sometimes the government, prevent competition so as to remain the sole producer of the good.

The demand curve for a monopolist is the industry's demand curve, as opposed to the horizontal demand curve faced by a perfectly competitive firm. The demand curve must slope downward because, in order to sell more output, the monopolist must lower the price of its product. Since the demand curve is also the average revenue curve and it slopes downward, the marginal revenue curve must lie below it. In other words, in order to sell more output, the monopolist must lower the price of all its output, not just the last unit he is selling (unless the monopolist practices price discrimination which shall be explained later in Section 5.4). So this affects the revenue he gets from each unit. The more numerous, low-priced, and close the substitutes are, the more elastic is the demand curve that the monopolist will face. The marginal revenue curve is given by:

$$MR = AR - \frac{AR}{\eta} = P\left(1 - \frac{1}{\eta}\right)$$

where $0 < \eta < \infty$ (we retain the negative sign for elasticity given that it reflects the slope of the demand curve).

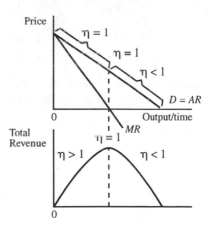

Figure 5.1

The monopolist will never produce in the inelastic portion of his demand curve because total revenue is declining in that area. The *MR* curve associated with a straight-line demand function always connects the demand function's vertical intercept with a point midway between the origin and the demand function's horizontal intercept.

Note: There is no supply curve for the monopolist because:

1. The output produced by a monopoly depends upon the position and slope of the demand, and

2. Any single monopoly price can result in a variety of rates of quantity produced.

Problem Solving Examples:

 What is a monopoly?

 A monopoly is a firm which is the sole producer of a good. A monopolist's power involves the control of the supply of this good to a degree sufficient to fix its price and prevent competition in its sale.

In a monopoly, since there is only one supplier, the industry's demand curve and the monopolist's demand curve are one and the same. In perfect competition, industry demand is ordinarily downward sloping while individual firm demand is perfectly elastic. Here the monopolist's (industry) demand curve is downward sloping.

 Given the following demand schedule for a monopolistic firm, plot the demand curve and the marginal revenue curve.

Quantity	Price
1	$30.00
2	$26.75
3	$23.50
4	$20.25
5	$17.00
6	$13.75

 To compute the marginal revenue, first find total revenue (price × quantity). Marginal revenue is equal to the change in total revenue as quantity is increased.

Quantity	Price	Total Revenue	Marginal Revenue
1	$30.00	$30.00	$30.00
2	$26.75	$53.50	$23.50
3	$23.50	$70.50	$17.00
4	$20.25	$81.00	$10.50
5	$17.00	$85.00	$ 4.00
6	$13.75	$82.50	$–2.50

To graph the demand and marginal revenue curves, we simply plot points, noticing that as quantity increases by 1, price decreases by $3.25 and marginal revenue decreases by $6.50. Therefore slope of demand = –3.25 and slope of marginal revenue = –6.50.

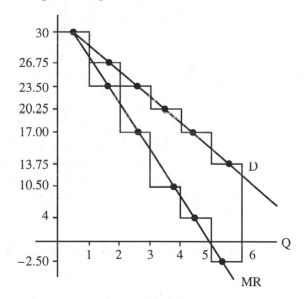

Remember that in perfect competition, the demand curve is a horizontal line; therefore, MR = Demand. But in monopoly, demand is downward-sloping, so MR is also downward-sloping, but with an even steeper slope.

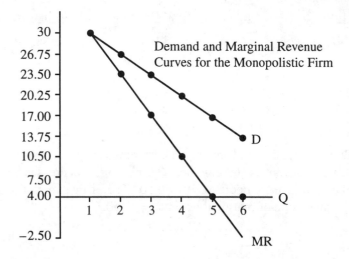

To see why MR is steeper than Demand, examine where they originate and examine the behavior of the two graphs, At Q = 0, TR = 0. Therefore at Q = 1, Price = TR = MR. But when Q > 1, price falls. And if price is falling, the new lower price must apply to all units sold. In our example at Q = 1, P = $30.00, while at Q = 2, P = $26.75. Now by selling 2 items, we gain $26.75 from the sale of the second item, but lose $3.25 ($30.00 – $26.75) on the first item which could have originally been sold for $30.00. Therefore MR = $26.75 – $3.25 = $23.50. This pattern will continue throughout the curves and MR will always be steeper than Demand.

5.2   Monopoly and Profit Maximization

The monopolist, like the competitive firm, wishes to maximize the difference between total revenue and total cost.

5.2.1   Short Run Monopoly Equilibrium

In the short run the monopolist must at least cover its variable cost. Again profits are maximized where the slope of the total revenue (*TR*) curve is equal to the slope of the total cost (*TC*) curve.

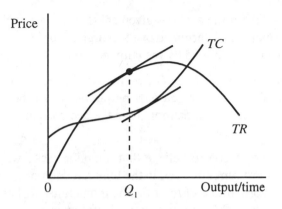

Figure 5.2

Note: Profits are not necessarily maximized where the total revenue is maximized.

The slope of the short run total cost curve is equal to the short run marginal cost curve and the slope of the total revenue curve is equal to the marginal revenue curve. Again, profit maximization in the short run occurs where:

$$MR = SRMC$$

Π - maximization short run

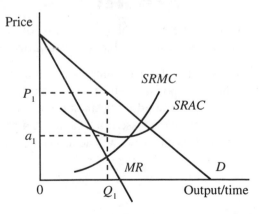

Figure 5.3

Total profits for the analysis given are $(P_1 - a_1) \times Q_1$. Note that the equilibrium output is determined by the marginal curves while the equilibrium price is determined by the demand curve.

If output increased above Q_1, cost would increase more than revenue and profits would decrease. If output decreased below Q_1, then the loss in revenue would be more than the decrease in cost and again profits would decrease.

There is no reason to believe that a monopolist always makes a profit in the short run (however, in the long run the monopolist must at least make a normal rate of return). The monopolist will at least try to minimize his loss. This can be seen in the following graph.

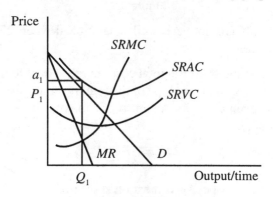

Figure 5.4

In the above graph, the monopolist takes a loss of $(a_1 - P_1) \times Q_1$ but is still able to operate because it is able to cover variable cost.

A price increase will not always increase the monopolist's profits. This is because the monopolist produces in the elastic part of the demand curve, unless the demand curve facing the monopolist is perfectly inelastic. As already discussed in Chapter 1, a price increase in the elastic part of the demand curve will actually decrease profits (See Section 1.9.5).

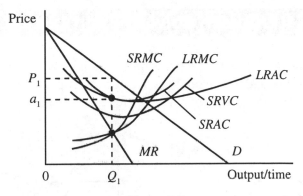

Figure 5.5

A monopolist may not always produce at the optimum rate of output in the optimum scale of the plant. We can see this in the above graph.

We know (see Section 4.4) that the optimum rate of output in the optimum scale of plant occurs where

$$SRMC = LRMC = MR = SRAC = LRAC.$$

However, in the case shown above, we have

$$SRMC = LRMC = MR < SRAC = LRAC.$$

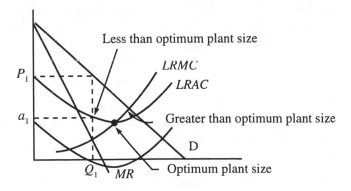

Figure 5.6

Therefore, we can see that a monopolist produces at less than optimum plant size.

Problem Solving Example:

Q Graphs (a) and (b) demonstrate a monopoly making normal profits and a monopoly producing at its point of maximum efficiency. Decide which graph applies for each situation.

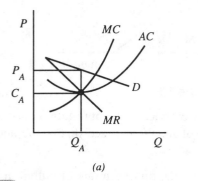

(a)

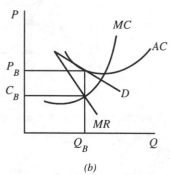

(b)

A This problem is asking for an interpretation of the two graphs. It is given that one represents a monopoly earning normal profits (no excess profits), and the other shows a monopoly producing at maximum efficiency (where average costs are minimized). Beginning with graph (a) at $MC = MR$, the profit maximization monopolist will produce Q_A units of output at a price of P_A. Note that at this intersection of MC and MR, the MC also intersects AC. Recall now that MC intersects AC only at the minimum point on the AC curve. Therefore, by producing an output of Q_A, at the point of minimum average costs, the monopolist in graph (a) is at maximum efficiency. A profit of C_A P_A per unit is being earned.

In graph (b), $MC = MR$ when output is Q_B. The corresponding price for this output is P_B, which is also the average cost when output is Q_B. Therefore, since price = average cost, the monopolist in graph (b) is earning only normal profits.

The reader should be warned at this point that the two situations shown above are not likely to occur in the real world. They illustrate two special cases, where profit maximization just happens to occur jointly with maximum efficiency or normal profits. Normally a monopolist will incur above-minimum average costs and earn higher-than-normal profits.

5.3 Natural Monopolies to Entry

5.3.1 Natural Monopolies

In some industries perfect competition is impractical or impossible because of economies of scale, i.e., increasing returns to scale. This situation results in a continuously declining cost curve over the relevant portion of output which causes a *natural monopoly.*

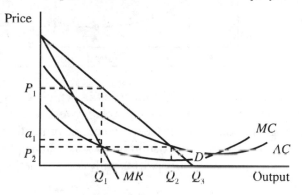

Figure 5.7

It is considered a natural monopoly because if another firm tries to enter the industry, the original firm can increase output and decrease price at Q_2 and P_2. The new firm cannot produce the remainder of the market, Q_2Q_3, at a price below P_2. So the new firm will leave the industry and prices will rise again.

A natural monopoly arises when AC_{min} of production of some good occurs at an output level that is sufficient for a single firm to supply a full market at an all cost inclusive price. This happens in cases of the economies of scale, where it is not profitable for more than one firm to exist in an industry because only one firm will be able to make a normal rate of return. A firm will continue to lower price and increase output until it drives all others out of business.

Problem Solving Example:

 What are natural monopolies?

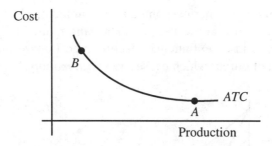

 Natural monopolies are industries in which competition is impractical, inconvenient, or simply unworkable.

The primary reason justifying the existence and promotion of natural monopolies is the existence of economies of scale. In a natural monopoly, the average total cost curve will usually look something like the curve in the figure.

Suppose the curve represents ATC for an electric company in a large city, where by having one firm produce at point *A*, all demand is satisfied. Now suppose the city government decided to break up this natural monopoly into five smaller companies of equal sizes. This would place each of the five companies at point *B* on the average cost curve, which represents considerably higher average cost. Thus, by allowing natural monopolies to exist, an economy is able to produce at a lower cost.

As a result of these considerations, the government will usually grant an exclusive franchise to a single firm when a tendency toward natural monopoly exists. Examples of this would be water, electricity, natural gas, and telephone service. However, in return for this gift of non-competition from the government, natural monopolies are subject to price control. This is necessary to prevent the natural monopolist from earning monopoly profits by restricting output and charging a high price.

5.3.2 Types of Barriers

Not all monopolies are natural monopolies. A monopoly with economic profit in the long run will generate the desire in others to enter the industry; therefore, a monopoly implies a need to put up barriers to remain the only one in the industry.

Types of Barriers:

1. Legal—directly prohibiting entry.

2. Patents/copyrights.

3. Trademarks/brand names.

4. Economies of scale—natural monopolies.

Barriers to entry are rarely complete; hence, monopolies are rare in pure form.

5.3.3 Measuring Monopoly Market Power

The **Lerner Index** of monopoly power $= \dfrac{P - MC}{P}$, where P = price of the good and MC = marginal cost of producing that good. This index measures the degree of monopoly power.

Problem Solving Example:

Why are barriers to entry important to a monopoly? Give some examples.

 The key element in preserving a monopoly is keeping potential rivals out of the market. One possibility is that some specific impediment prevents the establishment of a new firm in the industry. These impediments are called barriers to entry by economists.

Some examples:

• Legal restrictions—For example, private companies that might want to compete with the postal service are prohibited from doing so by law.

- Patents/copyrights—to encourage inventiveness, the government gives exclusive production rights for a period of time to the inventor of certain products. For example, Xerox had for many years a monopoly in plain paper copying.
- Technical superiority—a firm whose technological expertise vastly exceeds potential competitors' can, for a period of time, maintain a monopoly condition. For example, IBM for many years had little competition in the computer business.
- Economies of scale—mere size may provide cost advantages for some companies over smaller rivals.

5.4 Price Discrimination

5.4.1 Forms of Price Discrimination

Price Discrimination occurs when output is sold at different prices to different consumers so that the price differences do not reflect cost differentials; or in other instances charging the same price for goods that have different marginal cost.

Conditions for Price Discrimination:

1. The existence of a monopoly (or at least monopoly power to regulate prices).

2. The ability to segregate consumers with different elasticities of demand.

3. The original buyer cannot resell the good; prices in a low price region would go up to black-market levels.

Forms of Price Discrimination:

1. **Third-Degree Price Discrimination**: Different prices are charged for different markets (e.g., senior citizen discounts at the movies). Normally third-degree price discrimination just breaks the market up into a few different sub-markets.

2. **Second-Degree Price Discrimination:** As more and more of a good is purchased, its per unit price falls; a case of a declining rate schedule. An example of this would be bulk utility rates.

3. **First-Degree Price Discrimination:** A monopolist is able to obtain the full value that any single buyer places on each unit of his good.

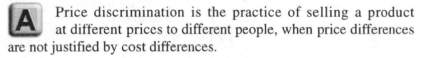

Problem Solving Example:

 What is price discrimination? How does a monopoly situation often make price discrimination possible?

Price discrimination is the practice of selling a product at different prices to different people, when price differences are not justified by cost differences.

Since there is only one seller in a monopoly situation, consumers must accept the monopolist's price. The consumer may see that the price paid is not uniform, but he will buy the monopolist's product anyway since there are no other suppliers.

It is important to realize that a monopolist can practice price discrimination only if no customer can resell the monopolist's product. If the product could be resold, those paying less for the product could sell to those paying more, undercutting the monopolist. In general, reselling is not possible when the output consists of services, such as legal advice, or medical services.

5.4.2 Graphical Analysis of Price Discrimination

The most common form of price discrimination is third-degree. In our example, we will assume that the two different markets have different elasticities of demand and we shall ignore cost to make our analysis easier. Since cost is not a factor, it makes sense that the monopolist should sell to the market with the highest marginal revenue in order to increase his total revenue by the highest amount possible. Therefore, the monopolist will equate the marginal revenue between the two markets. This can be seen in the following graph. We reverse the horizontal axis for market 2 and we assume that $Q_1 + Q_2$ will be the quantity to be sold in the market.

The marginal revenue for each market is equal to Q_1. Total revenue will not increase if one unit is added to one market and one unit is taken away from another market. We can see that $P_2 > P_1$. If the elasticities of demand are equal, then:

$$MR_1 = P_1\left(1 - \frac{1}{\eta_1}\right) = MR_2 = P_2\left(1 - \frac{1}{\eta_2}\right)$$

Since $\eta_1 = \eta_2$ if elasticities are equal, then $P_1 = P_2$ and there is no price discrimination. As shown in the above formula, if price discrimination exists, then the price would be higher in the market with the less elastic demand.

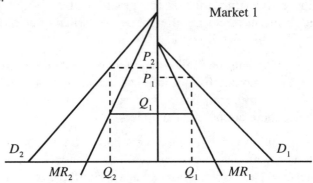

Figure 5.8 Third-Degree Price Discrimination

Second-degree price discrimination is also common. An example would be an electric company charging P_1 for the first 10,000 kilowatts, P_2 for the next 5,000 kilowatts, and P_3 for the next 5,000 kilowatts. This can be seen in the following graph.

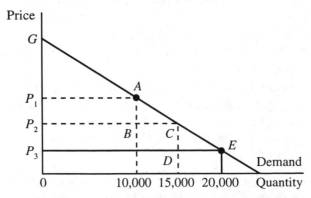

Figure 5.9 Second-Degree Price Discrimination

Without price discrimination the consumer would buy 20,000 kilowatts for a total cost of $P_3 \times 20,000$. However, with second-degree price discrimination, if the consumer desired to consume 20,000 kilowatts, he would have to pay $P_1 \times 10,000 + P_2 \times 5,000 + P_3 \times 5,000$ which is greater than $P_3 \times 20,000$. Without price discrimination, consumer surplus will be given by the area in the triangle GP_3E. With price discrimination, consumer surplus falls to $GP_1A + ABC + CDE$.

For first-degree price discrimination, the seller charges each buyer the highest price the buyer is willing to pay for that unit, and the seller charges a different price for each unit. Consumer surplus is wiped out and the producer gets all the surplus.

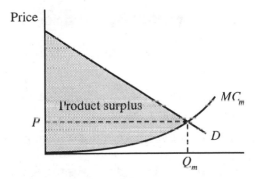

Figure 5.10 First-Degree Price Discrimination

5.5 The Multi-Plant Monopolist

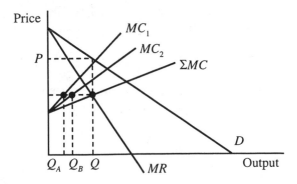

Figure 5.11

It is probable that a monopolist will use more than one plant to produce its output. In order for the monopolist to decide how much output to allocate between plants, the monopolist must add the marginal cost curves of the plants horizontally. The two plant case is depicted on the previous page.

The maximum profit output is where the sum of the marginal cost curves, ΣMC, is equal to the MR curve. From this point, we go back horizontally to determine how much each plant should produce. Plant 1 should produce Q_A and plant 2 should produce Q_B ($Q_A + Q_B = Q$).

5.6 Monopoly Resource Misallocation

5.6.1 Facts Concerning Monopoly Pricing

1. As in perfect competition, total profit, not profit-per-unit, is maximized.

2. Higher prices are not necessarily desirable due to the downward sloping demand.

3. Economic profits are not guaranteed to the monopolist.

5.6.2 Ways a Monopoly Produces Resource Misallocation

1. In a monopoly, most excess profits go to marketing rather than to research and development.

2. A monopoly contributes to income maldistribution as executives and stockholders take profits, thus making the rich richer.

3. For a monopolist, $P > MC$. This results in resource misallocation because the public pays more for a given good than its true cost. Not enough resources are going in to produce this good and it is going to less efficient uses in the economy. In other words, a mo-

nopoly causes a dead weight loss in consumer and producer surplus. This can be seen in the following graphs.

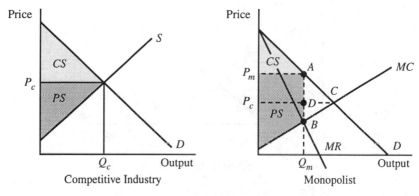

Figure 5.12

CS is consumer surplus and *PS* is producer surplus. In the case of a monopoly, $P_m > P_c$ and $Q_m < Q_c$, where P_m = price for monopolist, P_c = price for competitive industry, Q_m is quantity produced by monopolist, and Q_c is quantity produced by the competitive industry. Consumer surplus has fallen by $P_m A C P_c$, where $P_m A D P_c$ of this has been taken by the producer. The total increase in producer surplus is given by $P_m A D P_c - B D C$. However, we have a dead weight loss from the economy of ABC. This is the consequence of resource misallocation. More resources, and therefore output, should go into this industry because people value the output in this market more than the next best alternative.

5.7   Cartels and Collusion

Increasing Profits by Perfect Cartelization

Each firm's proportional demand in this industry is d_1 and its associated marginal revenue curve is *MR*. If we assume that the condition in this market is of perfect competition, then each firm will produce Q_c at a price of P_c ($P = MC$). If there are 1,000 firms in that industry, *TQ* will be $1,000 \times Q_c$.

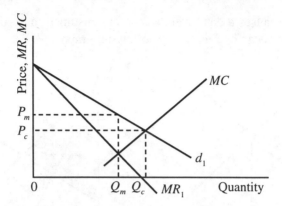

Figure 5.13

Assume: 1. All firms have identical costs.
2. All firms are of equal size.

Now, assume that a single agency which controls P and Q produced by the whole industry (because that industry's member firms have colluded, thus forming a **cartel**) assigned the output $Q_m/1,000$ (if there are 1,000 member firms) and price P_m to each member firm. Monopoly profits will thus be made by each firm via **cartelization**, providing there will be no cheating by its members.

There is always an incentive to cheat by cartel members on cartel agreements.

A cartel will set industry Q at $Q_{industry}$ and price at P_{cartel} to max Π for each member firm. Assume Q_{cartel} is what each individual firm in this cartel is told to produce. ATC is C_0 and its Π is the waved area.

If one firm thinks that no other member will cheat on the cartel's agreement, it will take P_{cartel} as given but now it will raise its output to Q_0 from Q_{cartel}. By doing this, its ATC will lower to C_2 and its profits will go up to include all horizontally shaded areas as well as the waved area, but the price will still be P_{cartel}. Thus, there is always an incentive for a member firm to cheat in the cartel in order to increase its Π.

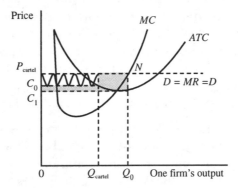

Figure 5.14

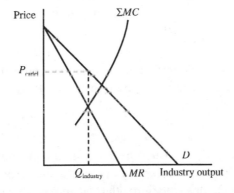

Problem Solving Examples:

 Explain the following as applied to oligopoly: cartel, gentlemen's agreements, price leadership.

 All three of the terms mentioned above describe a collusive situation in an oligopoly.

A cartel is by far the most blatant collusive arrangement of the three. Cartels are formal arrangements among producers to regulate price or output or to divide markets. Cartels are illegal in the United States. OPEC is an example of a cartel.

Gentlemen's agreements are more informal and subtle than cartels, and hence are undoubtedly widespread in our economy. Such agreements arise when competing oligopolists reach a verbal agreement on price or some other aspect of their strategies. Although they too collide with antitrust laws, gentlemen's agreements are difficult to detect and prosecute successfully due to their informal, sub rosa character.

Finally, price leadership is an even less formal means by which oligopolists coordinate their price behavior and avoid the uncertainty inherent in non-collusive action. In this case, one firm—usually the industry leader—initiates price changes, and all other firms more-or-less automatically follow that price change. Because price leadership is an informal, tacit agreement involving no written or spoken commitments, it is generally accepted as a legal technique by the courts in interpreting antitrust laws. The American steel industry is an example of a price leadership arrangement.

Q Suppose that the four firms in an oligopoly are getting together to collude. How might ease of entry into their industry affect how high they set their prices?

A Just because an industry is currently oligopolistic does not mean that it will remain so permanently. Suppose the four oligopolists above set their prices at an extremely high level and consequently earn a very large profit. In this situation, other businessmen will be tempted to enter this industry that shows such high profits. (Whereas before the collusion, profits were relatively low). If there is ease of entry, many businessmen will be attracted by the high-profit industry and hence, as the number of firms increase, our market structure will grow less and less oligopolistic. The ability to collude will also diminish.

The lesson to be learned is that if collusive price setting is to be practiced, care must be taken if it is easy for other firms to enter your industry. Specifically, prices should not be set so high as to create a profit which attracts too many new entrants. If this rule should be disobeyed, your oligopoly might soon exist no more and collusion becomes impossible due to the multitude of producers.

CHAPTER 6

Monopolistic Competition
and Oligopolies

6.1 Monopolistic Competition: Characteristics

Most real-world industries are neither perfectly competitive nor monopolistic, but a combination of the two.

Monopolistic Competition is a form of imperfect competition with the following characteristics:

1. Large number of sellers.

2. Product differentiation (either physical or perceived) gives some control over price since the product is heterogeneous. This leads to non-price competition such as advertising.

   Note: The true goal of advertising is to shift the demand curve to the right.

3. Relatively free entry and exit.

Product Group—A group of firms producing similar but not the same product.

Note: A perfectly competitive industry can become one that is monopolistically competitive if product differentiation is introduced through advertising or actual product differences.

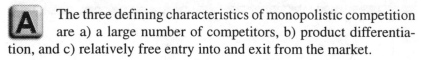

Problem Solving Examples:

 List the three main characteristics of monopolistic competition and discuss briefly the implications of these characteristics.

The three defining characteristics of monopolistic competition are a) a large number of competitors, b) product differentiation, and c) relatively free entry into and exit from the market.

The large number of competitors limits the control any individual firm has over market price. It also prevents price-fixing because of the difficulties involved in getting a large number of firms to act together. Monopolistic competition does not require the presence of hundreds of firms but only a fairly large number—say between 25 and 70.

Product differentiation gives each firm some control over the price of its products since consumers no longer perceive rivals' product as identical. That is, product differentiation gives the firm something of a monopoly where there are many close substitutes. Product differentiation also leads to nonprice competition among firms. This competition can focus on advertising or it can focus on the quality and workmanship of the competing products.

Ease of entry simply prevents firms from maintaining excess profits year after year. Suppose a firm is making extraordinary profits. If barriers to entry are low, other firms will soon enter the industry since it appears so lucrative. As new firms enter the market, profits will be reduced to "normal" levels.

Q What is a product group?

A "Product group" is the term Edward Chamberlin, one of the most famous theorists on monopolistic competition, used to describe a group of firms producing similar, but not identical, products. In other words, it is his name for a monopolistically competitive industry. He used this term to try to defend his theory against the criticism that monopolistically competitive industries could not be adequately defined, since all of the firms produce different products. Chamberlin asserted that meaningful classifications of industries could be made.

6.2 Monopolistic Competition: Demand and Profit Maximization in the Short Run

The monopolistic firm assumes that it does have some amount of monopoly power. Therefore, it perceives its demand curve as being negatively sloping. This implies that a decrease in the price of a given good leads to an increase in demand for its particular brand of product. Thus, $MC = MR < P = AR = D$ in order to maximize profits.

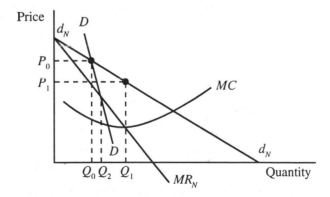

Figure 6.1 The Firm and Industry Demand in the Monopolistic Competitive Market

$d_N d_N$ → perceived firm demand

DD → share of the market curve shows how output for the firm changes as all other firms match the decline in price.

d_N is drawn assuming:

1. All firms are of equal size.

2. Price charged by each firm is the same.

At P_0 a firm will sell Q_0. Each firm thinks that its demand is $d_N d_N$, assuming that every other firm will keep its price at P_0. However, the firm is not maximizing profits at Q_0 because $MR \neq MC$. The firm then attempts to sell Q_1 units of output where $MC = MR$ by lowering its price from P_0 to P_1. However, this price and quantity is not attainable because once the firm lowers its price to $P_1 Q$ all other firms will match the decline in price and increase in output. Therefore, the firm's "real" demand curve is DD and at P_1 it will produce only Q_2 units of output.

The Monopolistic Competition and the Short Run Equilibrium

In time, Q^* will be located where $MC = MR_N$ and at that same quantity, the share of market demand curve will intersect the perceived demand curve, $d_N d_N$. This is shown in the following graph.

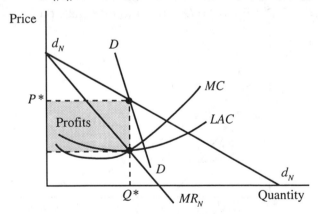

Figure 6.2 Monopolistic Competition and Short Run Equilibrium

Problem Solving Examples:

 Does the graph show a potential profit-maximizing equilibrium point for a monopolistic competitor? Why or why not?

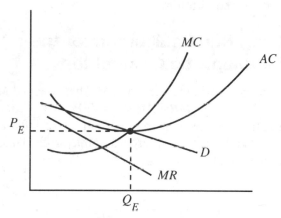

 The profit maximizing condition for any firm is to produce at the quantity where $MR = MC$. The firm in the diagram can be identified as a monopolistic competitor by its highly elastic, downward sloping demand curve. Using the diagram in the question, note that this firm has chosen to produce at the minimum average cost level, Q_E, with its associated price, P_E, where no excess profit is earned. (At Q_E, the AC curve is exactly equal to the demand, or AR curve.) Note that if this firm were to decrease its production to Q_M where $MR = MC$, and increase its price to P_M, as shown,

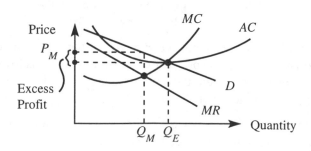

excess profits could be earned. (At Q_M, the AC curve lies below the AR curve, with the distance between the two representing the excess profit per unit.) Therefore, since Q_M, with its associated price of P_M, not Q_E, with price P_E, is the profit-maximizing point for this monopolistic competitor, the diagram given in the question does not correctly show a profit-maximizing equilibrium.

6.3 Long Run Equilibrium for the Monopolistic Competitor

In the long run, as in the short run, MC has to equal MR to maximize profits. Thus, $MC = MR < AR = D = P$. Positive economic profits will cause entry into the industry. DD will move leftwards in time, causing individual firms to earn zero economic profit. This can be seen in the following graph.

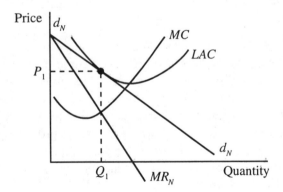

**Figure 6.3 Long Run Equilibrium for the
Monopolistic Competitive Firm**

In monopolistic competition, $P > MC$ in the long run so that the monopolistic competition prices are higher and output is lower than in perfect competition, where they are at their optimal level. Thus, there is inefficiency in monopolistic competition.

Note: In equilibrium, perfect competition in the long run produces on the minimum point of its long run average cost ($LRAC$) curve. This is not the case for short run and long run equilibrium of monopolistic competition. This is due to the fact that the monopolistic competitor faces a downward sloping demand curve, whereas the perfect competitor faces a horizontal demand curve.

Society's resources are not being utilized sufficiently, which always occurs when $P > MC$. Not enough of society's resources are employed and not enough output is produced to get to the *LRAC* minimum point.

Problem Solving Example:

 Could the following diagram represent a long run equilibrium for a monopolistic competitor? Why or why not?

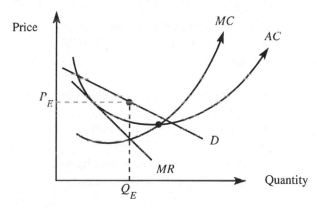

In the long run, because of the free entry and exit assumption, all of the monopolistic competitor's excess profits are assumed to be competed away. That is, if, in the short run, the monopolistic competitor is earning excess profits, new firms will enter the industry, decreasing the demand for the original firm's product, and raising costs to the original firm. If, in the short run, a monopolistically competitive industry is incurring losses, many of its firms may decide to leave the industry, decreasing costs and increasing demand to the remaining firms. Thus, in the long run, all excess profits are assumed to be competed to zero.

In the diagram, note that at Q_E, the profit-maximizing output level, the *AC* curve lies below the *AR* curve. That is, at this point, the given firm is earning excess profits. Therefore, the given diagram does not show a long run equilibrium point for a monopolistic competitor.

6.4   Oligopoly: Defined

An **Oligopoly** is a market structure that is characterized by a few sellers of goods which are close substitutes. The price charged by one firm in the industry is considered by all other firms when they make their pricing decisions. There are many models which describe an oligopoly's output and pricing decisions, each based on different assumptions.

Problem Solving Examples:

Q Suppose we are told that an industry is composed of a small number of firms. Can we immediately call this industry oligopolistic? Explain.

A The term "oligopoly" literally means "few sellers." However, it is not the actual number of sellers that is important in studying oligopoly. Rather it is the existence of interactions between the sellers that concern us in studying oligopoly. A market has an oligopolistic structure if actions by one firm have such important effects upon rivals that these rivals will contemplate appropriate reactions, which may affect the original firm. In other words, an oligopoly exists when each firm in an industry must contemplate the possible reactions of its rivals in deciding its own behavior.

Q What is the difference between a homogeneous and a differentiated oligopoly?

A In a homogeneous oligopoly, the firms produce standardized products, that is, the consumer perceives the different firms' products as being essentially the same. Examples of homogeneous oligopolies would be the steel and lead industries.

In differentiated oligopolies, products are no longer perceived by the consumer as being the same. Examples of differentiated oligopolies would be the automobile and cigarette industries.

Notice the emphasis of the word "perception" above. In some instances of differentiated oligopoly, the degree of difference perceived by consumers is far greater than the real difference that exists between products.

6.5 Oligopoly: Classical Models

If all firms in the industry would work together, they would attempt to maximize total (industry) profits. This is given where the marginal cost curve intersects the marginal revenue curve for the industry.

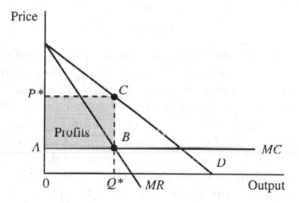

Figure 6.4

If we assume costs are constant, the most profit this industry can extract is given by the rectangle $P*ABC$.

6.5.1 Cournot's Model

Cournot assumes that each firm will take its rival's output as fixed and base its own output decision on that. This can be seen in the following graph. To make our analysis easier, we will assume that marginal cost is equal to zero.

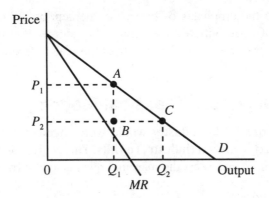

Figure 6.5

If Firm I is the only firm in the industry, it would produce for one-half of the market and its profit would be OP_1AQ_1. As Firm II enters the industry, one-half of the market is not supplied, Q_1D. Firm II now maximizes its profit by producing one-half of the remainder of the market, Q_1D_1, or one-fourth of the market, Q_1Q_2. Firm I now sees its profits drop to OP_2BQ_1. Firm I now assumes that Firm II will continue to produce Q_1Q_2 and Firm I will now make its output decision given Firm II's output. So Firm I will now produce $\frac{1}{2}(1-\frac{1}{4}) = \frac{3}{8}$. It is now time for Firm II to react—Firm II will produce $\frac{1}{2}(1-\frac{3}{8}) = \frac{5}{16}$. This process will continue until the market is in equilibrium where each firm produces $\frac{1}{3}$, $\frac{1}{2}(1-\frac{1}{3}) = \frac{1}{3}$ for each firm. (Note: The two firms are not maximizing industry profits.)

We can view this in terms of reaction curves given in Figure 6.6.

In the reaction function, one firm is passive while the other firm reacts. Let's look at II's reaction function. If I produces 1, then Firm II will produce nothing. If Firm I produces nothing, Firm II will produce $\frac{1}{2}$. If Firm I produces $\frac{1}{2}$, Firm II will produce $\frac{1}{4}$. When Firm I produces $\frac{1}{3}$, Firm II produces $\frac{1}{3}$. The equilibrium point is given where the two reaction functions intersect. At this point no firm has the incentive to change its output.

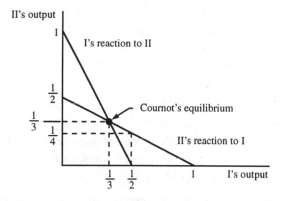

Figure 6.6 Cournot's Reaction Functions

6.5.2 Bertrand's Model

Bertrand's model differs from Cournot's model in that Bertrand assumes that each firm takes its rival's prices as fixed and not their output. Therefore, prices will be cut until it reaches the competitive level. Each will lower price to gain a larger share in the market. This can easily be seen by using price reaction functions.

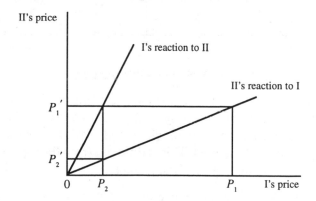

Figure 6.7 Bertrand's Reaction Functions

If Firm I sets its price at P_1, then Firm II will set its price at P_1'. As Firm II sets its price at P_1', Firm I will react and set its price at P_2. Again it is time for Firm II to react and it will set its price at P_2'. This will continue until we reach $P = P' = D$, the competitive price.

6.5.3 Edgeworth's Model

The main assumption in Edgeworth's model is that each firm has limited productive ability and cannot service the entire market. Another assumption in Edgeworth's model is that each firm selects a price by assuming that its rival will keep its price constant.

We will assume that the maximum quantity for each firm is $Q_{1\,max}$ and $Q_{2\,max}$ for Firm I and Firm II, respectively.

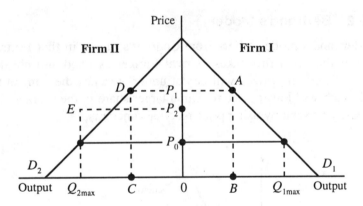

Figure 6.8 Edgeworth's Duopoly Model

For simplicity, let us assume that each firm is confronted with its own demand curve made of one-half of all workers. If the two firms worked together, Firm I would sell $0B$ and Firm II would sell $0C$, $0B = 0C = \frac{1}{4}$ of the total market. This is different from the Cournot solution of each firm producing $\frac{1}{3}$ of the market.

If they do not work together, one might cut its price to increase its profit. If Firm I charges P_1, Firm II can increase its profit from P_1DC0 to $P_2EQ_{2\,max}0$, if it slightly cuts its price from P_1 to P_2. Since Firm II has the lowest price, all customers will buy from him until he reaches his maximum production and the rest of the customers will buy from Firm I. But now Firm I will retaliate by lowering its price below P_2. This will continue until both produce the most they can at P_Q (assuming $Q_{1\,max} = Q_{2\,max}$). However, this price is not a stable one. Firm I can slightly increase its price and not worry about losing profits, because Firm II is already producing the most it can and the other half of the market would be willing to be served at any price. And given that the producer is producing in the inelastic part of his demand curve, BD_1, he can increase profits by increasing price. Firm I will raise prices up to P_1 and gain monopoly profits. However, Firm II will follow and the process will start over again. Therefore, there is no stable equilibrium in Edgeworth's model.

6.6   Sweezy's Kinked Demand Curve

Assumptions:

1. Firms in the industry are rational.

2. Rival firms quickly match price reductions.

3. Rival firms slowly and rarely match price increases.

We will assume that price is initially at P_E, the equilibrium price. This price is not given or explained by the theory.

Above the equilibrium price, the demand curve facing the firm is very elastic since sales will fall off sharply and because others will not follow price rise. Below the equilibrium price the demand curve is very inelastic because the other firms will match the price cut. Quantity still increases as price falls but not nearly as rapidly as would be if other firms did not lower their prices. Thus, the upper portion of the demand curve is the usual Marshallian demand curve, while the lower portion of the demand curve is the share of the market curve. The difference in the slope of the two depends upon the percentage of the market the firm has.

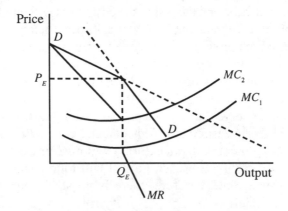

Figure 6.9 The Kinked Demand Curve

Note: In the area where *MR* is discontinuous, small changes in *MC* are ignored by the oligopolist. He continues to produce at Q_E and P_E, where *MC = MR,* to maximize his profits.

Problem Solving Example:

 Explain the rationale behind the kinked demand curve used by economists to describe oligopoly.

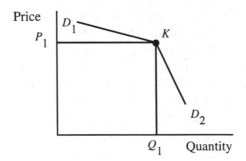

In order to explain demand in an oligopoly, economists use a kinked demand curve, such as illustrated in the figure.

The kinked demand curve is used to explain the price inflexibility that characterizes oligopoly. Let us consider the price strategy of an oligopolist selling Q_1 units of output at price = P_1. This point (k) is called the kink.

If the oligopolist lowers his price, his competitors will follow suit and lower their prices also. Therefore, the curve shows that as he lowers price, quantity demanded increases very slowly. As price falls along this inelastic portion of the curve, the oligopolist's total revenue ($P \times Q$) will fall. On the other hand, if the oligopolist raises his price, his competitors will most likely not raise their prices. When this happens, the high-priced product will no longer be so attractive to the customer and quantity demanded will drop a great deal. Here, the demand curve is highly elastic, that is, by increasing his prices, the oligopolist's total revenue will decline. Therefore, according to the kinked demand curve, it does not pay for the oligopolist to raise or lower prices.

6.7 Non-Price Competition and Implicit Collusion

Price competition is seldom seen in the oligopolistic industry where prices are usually stable. This is because price competition will erode away pure profits. Non-price competition is the alternative that is frequently observed as a method of increasing market share by a firm. Non-price competition includes advertising and other methods of product differentiation, such as customer service. Since we see stable prices in an oligopolistic industry, prices must be set in some way. There are two main forms of non-explicit cartel arrangement in the industry:

1. Price-leadership by the low-cost firm in the industry.

2. Price-leadership by the dominant firm in the industry.

6.7.1 The Low-Cost Firm Price Leadership Model

To best show this model, let's assume that there are just two firms in the industry with unequal cost. This situation is depicted by the graph below.

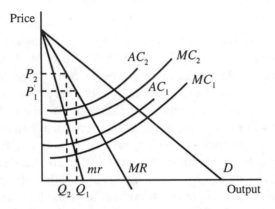

Figure 6.10 Low-Cost Firm Price Leadership Model

Let us further assume that the two firms equally share the market and Firm II has higher costs than Firm I. Since the market (D) is split in half, each firm faces demand curve d which used to be the marginal revenue curve. But now the marginal revenue curve faced by each firm is given by mr. Firm II wishes to maximize profits where its marginal cost curve intersects its marginal revenue curve. This is at quantity Q_2 and price P_2. However, since Firm I has lower cost, it maximizes profits at quantity Q_1 and price P_1. Obviously, the low-cost firm will prevail and both firms will produce Q_1 and sell it at P_1. Note that at this quantity Firm II is not maximizing its profits although it is still making some pure profits.

6.7.2 The Dominant Firm Price Leadership Model

This model assumes that one firm is so large that it can set a price and let all other firms sell all they want at this price. The dominant firm then sells to the rest of the market. This model is depicted in the following graph.

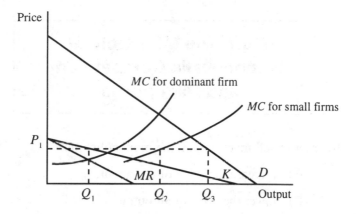

Figure 6.11 Dominant Firm Price Leadership Model

D is the market demand for the industry. The difference between ΣMC and D gives d, the amount the dominant firm can sell at various prices. ΣMC gives us the supply curve for the sum of all small firms in the industry. The dominant firm derives its MR curve from its demand curve and maximizes where $MC = MR$ at Q_1 and P_1. At price P_1, all the small firms act competitively and sell all they can at this price, Q_2. The total sold on this market is Q_3, $Q_1 + Q_2 = Q_3$.

In conclusion, it should be noted that there exists no general theory of oligopoly, but only models of specific situations describing possible behavior patterns.

Problem Solving Example:

 What is the relationship of price leadership to collusion?

An example of tacit collusion is price leadership, an arrangement in which one firm in the industry is, in effect, assigned the task of making pricing decisions for the entire group. It is expected that other firms in the industry will adopt the prices set by the price leader. Typically, the price setter will be the dominant firm in that industry, e.g., it has been suggested that for many years, steel prices came under the price leadership of U.S. Steel and at times Bethlehem Steel.

Quiz: The Monopoly & Monopolistic Competition and Oligopolies

1. In order to sell more output, the monopolist must

    (A) increase the price of all output.

    (B) lower the price of all output.

    (C) keep the price constant for all output.

    (D) None of the above.

2. Monopoly short run profit maximization is realized when

    (A) $MR = MC$.

    (B) $MR = AC$.

    (C) $MR = TC$.

    (D) None of the above.

3. All but one of the following are barriers to entry that help explain the existence of monopoly. Which is not such a barrier?

    (A) Economies of scale

    (B) Control of essential raw materials

    (C) Patent ownership

    (D) Highly inelastic demand

    (E) Unfair competitive practices

4. The Lerner Index of monopoly power is

  (A) $\dfrac{P - AC}{P}$.

  (B) $\dfrac{P - MC}{P}$.

  (C) $\dfrac{P - TC}{P}$.

  (D) None of the above.

5. Price discrimination takes place when

  (A) a given product is sold at more than one price and these price differences are not justified by cost differences.

  (B) different prices, to compensate for differences in the characteristics of the product, are charged.

  (C) the price is equal to the per unit cost of the product.

  (D) increased price lowers the supply of the product.

6. Which of the following is a characteristic of oligopoly?

  (A) A market situation with only a few competing buyers

  (B) A market situation with only a few competing sellers

  (C) A market situation with only one seller

  (D) An open market for the best interests of the consumer

  (E) Government control of prices

7. Cournot's model assumes that each firm will take its rival's output as fixed and base its own

    (A) pricing decision on that.

    (B) output decision on that.

    (C) input decision on that.

    (D) All of the above.

8. Economists are not very interested in non-collusive oligopoly as they are in collusive oligopoly because

    (A) gentlemen's agreements are not widespread in the economy.

    (B) there is no intra-industry competition.

    (C) it does not provide a more satisfactory explanation of price and output behavior.

    (D) of the uncertainties about the behavior of other firms in the industry.

9. In the most standard usage, the term "price leadership" refers to

    (A) preemptive pricing made possible by the learning curve.

    (B) a form, in effect, of price collusion.

    (C) the maintenance of a monopolistic price.

    (D) cutthroat competition.

10. Prices are likely to be least flexible under

    (A) pure competition.

    (B) oligopoly.

    (C) monopolistic competition.

    (D) monopoly.

ANSWER KEY

1.	(B)	6.	(B)
2.	(A)	7.	(B)
3.	(D)	8.	(C)
4.	(B)	9.	(B)
5.	(A)	10.	(B)

CHAPTER 7

Factor Prices

7.1 Forms of Income Generation

Income comes from three main sources:

1. Wages (W)—The price charged by a worker for his/her services.

2. Rent—The price charged for the use of land (L) or for capital (K).

3. Transfers—Income from the government or other sources such as Social Security that the person receives but gives nothing in return.

The factors of production command prices. This chapter will discuss how these prices are established and its significance on the profits and cost of the firms which hire them.

7.2 Perfect Competition in the Resource Market

Perfect Competition in the Resource Market means that a single firm can hire as much of an input as it desires, yet has no effect on the price of that input; no resource supplier is so large that it can influence its price; and resources are freely mobile.

Least Cost Rule—The cost of output is minimized when the marginal product of the last dollar spent for each input is equated.

$$\frac{MP_a}{P_a} = \frac{MP_b}{P_b}$$

However, this just tells us the least cost way of producing a given output and not the profit maximizing level, that is, it just gives us a point on the long run average cost curve. We may define P_A/MP_A as the "change in cost due to a change in output." This is the same as the marginal cost. Therefore, $MP_A/P_A = 1/MC_A$. Now to maximize profits, marginal revenue must equal marginal cost. In a competitive industry we know that $P = MR$. So the optimum level of output is given by:

$$\frac{MP_a}{P_a} = \frac{MP_b}{P_b} = \frac{1}{MC_A} = \frac{1}{P_A}$$

where P_A = Price of output
       P_a = Price of input

Graphically, this is shown below.

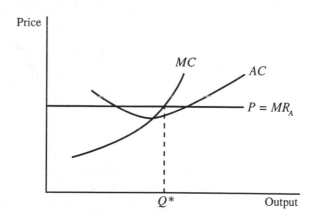

Figure 7.1

7.3 Resource Demand for a Competitive Buyer and Seller

The firm should use more of an input as long as the increase in total revenue from this input is greater than the increase in total cost, that is, $MR > MC$. Thus, the maximizing amount of input A is where:

$$\frac{MP_a}{P_a} = \frac{1}{P_A} \quad \text{and} \quad P_A \cdot MP_a = P_a$$

assuming input b is fixed. This means that the value of the marginal product of input a is equal to the price paid for a in a perfectly competitive market.

Quantity	P_A	MP_a	VMP_a	P_a	AP_a	ARP
0	3	0	0	12	0	0
1	3	2	6	12	2	6
2	3	4	12	12	3	9
3	3	6	18	12	4	12
4	3	7	21	12	4.75	14.25
5	3	6	18	12	5	15
6	3	4	12	12	4.83	14.49
7	3	3	9	12	4.57	13.71

Table 7.1

We can examine this condition with the help of the above table. According to the maximization condition, $P_A \times MP_a = P_a$, we will either hire two or six units of input a. However, note that at two units total revenue equals 18, (6 + 12), while total variable cost equals 24, (12 × 2). At six units, total revenue is equal to 87 (sum of the VMP_a's) while total cost is equal to 72 (12 × 6).

Obviously, six units of a should be hired instead of two. This can also be seen graphically as depicted below.

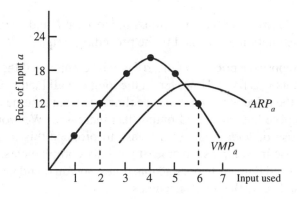

Figure 7.2

Notice that at six units, the average revenue product of $a(ARP_a)$ is greater than the value of the marginal product of $a(VMP_a)$, whereas at two units ARP_a is greater than VMP_a. Therefore, input a will be hired up to a point where $VMP_a = P_a$ and $ARP_a > P_a$. This will only happen when VMP_a is falling. Therefore, the downward sloping section of the VMP_a curve is the firm's input demand curve because at $12 the firm will demand six units of input a.

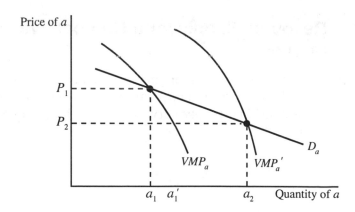

Figure 7.3

Now suppose the price of an input falls. The firm will substitute into the good which is now relatively cheaper. This is known as the **substitution rule**.

Suppose a firm is initially maximizing profits at P_1 and hiring quantity a_1. This situation is depicted in the preceding graph.

Now suppose the price of a falls; $a_1{'}$ will be employed if the amount of other inputs was fixed. However, in the long run all factors are variable. Since the price of the input has declined, we can assume the marginal cost curve has fallen and output has increased. We would also expect the use of *both* inputs to increase to produce this increase in output because most inputs are at least partially complements. For example, you need humans to operate machines, so you could never have a factory made completely of machines.

Since the use of input b has also increased slightly (but less than the increase in input a), the marginal product curve for a will also shift to the right. With the price of the output constant, the VMP_a curve will also shift to the right. Therefore, at P_2, a_2 units of input a will be employed instead of $a_1{'}$.

Therefore, the actual demand curve for input a in the long run (with all inputs variable) is given by D_a, and VMP_a is the short run demand curve.

7.4 Resource Supply for a Competitive Market

The market supply curve for an input is given by the horizontal summation of the individual supply curves of all the factors of the input. The individual supply curve is derived by indifference curve analysis.

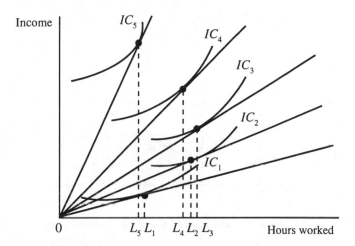

Figure 7.4 Derivation of Individual Supply of Input

The lines from the origin in the above graph give us the income received during the time period. The slope of the line gives the wage rate—the steeper the line, the higher the wage rate. The indifference curves (*IC*) give us points where the individual is indifferent about hours worked. The level of satisfaction increases as we move to the top left, assuming the individual considers income and leisure goods. It reflects the fact that to encourage a worker to work longer you must pay him more. The individual attempts to reach the highest indifference curves given the wage rate and indifference map structure. If we trace out these equilibrium points, we get a backward bending supply curve as depicted in Figure 7.5.

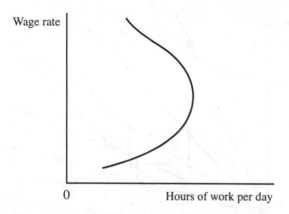

Wage rate

0   Hours of work per day

Figure 7.5 The Backward Bending Supply Curve

Not all individual supply curves are backward bending. It depends only on the shape of the individual's indifference curves. Also, this does not mean that the market supply curve is backward bending. Not all individual supply curves bend the same, but to have a backward bending supply curve at least one individual supply curve must bend backwards.

Problem Solving Example:

Explain the backward bending supply curve for labor drawn below.

In general, as wages rise, everything else being equal, the quantity of labor offered to the market will increase. This explains our supply curve up to point A. But then supply starts moving back-

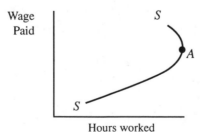

Wage Paid

S

A

S

Hours worked

wards. As wages are raised, our curve tells us that workers will work less hours. The reason for this is that as wages become extremely high, workers will be making so much money that they will no longer need to work a full week. Also, as salary increases, the attractiveness of leisure time will increase for the workers and labor hours supplied will decline.

7.5   Resource Demand for a Monopolist

The least-cost combination of factors is the same for the monopolist as the competitor, that is, $MP_a/P_a = MP_b/P_b$. However,

$$\frac{MP_a}{P_a} = \frac{MP_b}{P_b} > \frac{1}{MC_A} = \frac{1}{P_A}$$

is not the best profit position for the monopolist because the monopolist faces a downward sloping demand curve. If $MR_A > MC_A$, then we have

$$\frac{MP_a}{P_a} = \frac{MP_b}{P_b} = \frac{1}{MC_A} > \frac{1}{MR_A}$$

Thus, the monopolist is using the factors in the correct proportion, but not enough to maximize profits. The monopolist is in equilibrium when:

$$\frac{MP_a}{P_a} = \frac{MP_b}{P_b} = \frac{1}{MC_A} = \frac{1}{MR_A} > \frac{1}{P_A}$$

Therefore, the marginal revenue product of the input must equal its price.

$$MR_A \times MP_a = Pa$$
$$MR_A \times MP_a = MRP_a$$

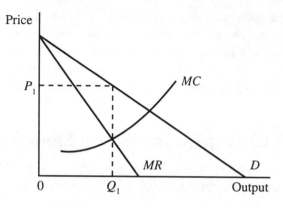

Figure 7.6

This means that a factor is hired up to the point where its addition to total revenue is equal to its addition to total cost.

However, for a monopolist the MRP_a is less than VMP_a, because the monopolist MR is less than P.

For the same reasons given for the competitive case in Section 7.3, we are only concerned with the downward sloping portion of the MRP_a curve, and again $P_a < ARP_a$.

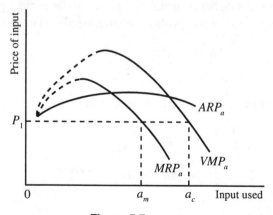

Figure 7.7

As can be seen by the above graph, the monopolist hires less than would be hired in a competitive market. The MRP_a curve, and not the VMP_a curve, is the demand curve for the monopolist.

7.6   The Monopsonist

A **monopsonist** is a single buyer in a market. A monopsony could occur because of specialization of that factor to a particular use or because of factor immobility. Since the monopsonist is the only buyer of the factor, he must pay a higher price to attract more workers. Therefore, he faces an upward-sloping supply curve. This situation is depicted in the following graph.

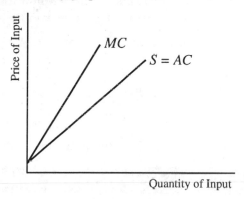

Figure 7.8

Since the average cost of the input is equal to the price of the input and it increases as the quantity increases, the marginal cost curve must be above the average cost curve.

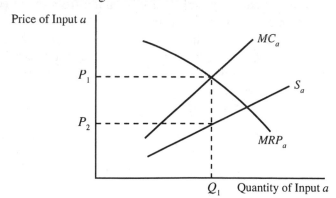

Figure 7.9

The same principle of profit maximization will apply to the monopsonist as was applied to others. That is, the monopsonist will equate the marginal revenue product of the input, MRP_a, to the additions to total cost by hiring more of this input MC_a (giving that $P_a \leq ARP_a$ as explained in Section 7.3). We can see this situation in Figure 7.9.

The firm will hire Q_1 because this is where $MRP_a = MC_a$. The monopsonist is paying P_2 per unit of input a, therefore, he is making a profit of $P_1 - P_2$ per unit of input he hires. This is called **exploitation** because the monopsonist pays the factor less than its contribution.

Since $MC_a > P_a$, the least-cost criterion $MP_a/P_a = MP_b/P_b$ is no longer correct. Instead, the least-cost criterion for the monopsonist is:

$$\frac{MP_a}{MC_a} = \frac{MP_b}{MC_b}$$

When this criterion is met, the monopsonist is on the *LRAC* curve.

Problem Solving Example:

What is the difference between monopoly and monopsony?

Both words contain the part "mono" coming from the Greek word for "one." Monopoly is the market situation in which there is only one seller. Monopsony is the market situation in which there is only one buyer. The model of perfect competition cannot be used to explain either of these situations since it assumes there are many buyers and many sellers in a market situation.

Quiz: Factor Prices

1. Perfect competition in the resource market means that a single firm can hire as much of an input as it desires yet has

    (A) little effect on the price of that input.

    (B) no effect on the price of that input.

    (C) significant effect on the price of that input.

    (D) None of the above.

2. The Least Cost Rule formula shows us the

    (A) profit-maximizing level.

    (B) the least cost way of producing a given output.

    (C) Both (A) and (B).

    (D) None of the above.

3. A firm should use more of an input as long as revenue from the input is greater than increase in costs or

    (A) $MR = MC$

    (B) $MR < MC$

    (C) $MR > MC$

    (D) None of the above.

4. A backward bending supply curve for labor is

   (A) not possible.

   (B) entirely possible.

   (C) dependent on output.

   (D) None of the above.

5. In a monopoly, the marginal revenue product of the input must

   (A) exceed its price.

   (B) be below its price.

   (C) equal its price.

   (D) None of the above.

6. A monopsony exists where there is

   (A) a single buyer in a market.

   (B) a single seller in a market.

   (C) few buyers and sellers in a market.

   (D) None of the above.

7. Because a monopsonist must pay a higher price to attract more workers, he faces

   (A) a downward sloping curve.

   (B) a horizontal supply curve.

   (C) an upward sloping supply curve.

   (D) None of the above.

8. In a monopsony the marginal cost curve of inputs must be

   (A) below the average cost curve.

(B)   equal to the average cost curve.

(C)   above the average cost curve.

(D)   None of the above.

9.   In a monopsonistic labor buying situation with no market imper-
fections, once the employer determines the level of employment
which will maximize profits (or minimize costs), he sets wages
as dictated by examining

(A)   demand for labor.

(B)   supply of labor.

(C)   substitutability of capital equipment for labor.

(D)   union requirements and government wage laws.

10.   A monopsonist maximizes profits by hiring workers up to the
point where marginal labor costs are

(A)   above the marginal revenue product.

(B)   below the marginal revenue product.

(C)   equal to the marginal revenue product.

(D)   None of the above.

ANSWER KEY

1.	(B)	6.	(A)
2.	(B)	7.	(C)
3.	(C)	8.	(C)
4.	(B)	9.	(B)
5.	(C)	10.	(C)

REA's Test Preps
The Best in Test Preparation

- REA "Test Preps" are **far more** comprehensive than any other test preparation series
- Each book contains up to **eight** full-length practice tests based on the most recent exams
- **Every** type of question likely to be given on the exams is included
- Answers are accompanied by **full** and **detailed** explanations

REA publishes over 70 Test Preparation volumes in several series. They include:

Advanced Placement Exams (APs)
Art History
Biology
Calculus AB & BC
Chemistry
Economics
English Language & Composition
English Literature & Composition
European History
French Language
Government & Politics
Latin
Physics B & C
Psychology
Spanish Language
Statistics
United States History
World History

College-Level Examination Program (CLEP)
Analyzing and Interpreting Literature
College Algebra
Freshman College Composition
General Examinations
General Examinations Review
History of the United States I, II
Introduction to Educational Psychology
Human Growth and Development
Introductory Psychology
Introductory Sociology
Precalculus
Principles of Management
Principles of Marketing
Spanish
Western Civilization I, II

SAT Subject Tests
Biology E/M
Chemistry
French
German
Literature
Mathematics Level 1, 2
Physics
Spanish
United States History

Graduate Record Exams (GREs)
Biology
Chemistry
Computer Science
General
Literature in English
Mathematics
Physics
Psychology

ACT - ACT Assessment

ASVAB - Armed Services Vocational Aptitude Battery

CBEST - California Basic Educational Skills Test

CDL - Commercial Driver License Exam

CLAST - College Level Academic Skills Test

COOP & HSPT - Catholic High School Admission Tests

ELM - California State University Entry Level Mathematics Exam

FE (EIT) - Fundamentals of Engineering Exams - For Both AM & PM Exams

FTCE - Florida Teacher Certification Examinations

GED - (U.S. Edition)

GMAT - Graduate Management Admission Test

LSAT - Law School Admission Test

MAT - Miller Analogies Test

MCAT - Medical College Admission Test

MTEL - Massachusetts Tests for Educator Licensure

NJ HSPA - New Jersey High School Proficiency Assessment

NYSTCE - New York State Teacher Certification Examinations

PRAXIS PLT - Principles of Learning & Teaching Tests

PRAXIS PPST - Pre-Professional Skills Tests

PSAT/NMSQT

SAT

TExES - Texas Examinations of Educator Standards

THEA - Texas Higher Education Assessment

TOEFL - Test of English as a Foreign Language

TOEIC - Test of English for International Communication

USMLE Steps 1,2,3 - U.S. Medical Licensing Exams

If you would like more information about any of these books,
complete the coupon below and return it to us or visit your local bookstore.

Research & Education Association
61 Ethel Road W., Piscataway, NJ 08854
Phone: (732) 819-8880   website: www.rea.com

Please send me more information about your Test Prep books.

Name _____

Address _____

City _____ State _____ Zip _____